ROADMAP TO STUDY ABROAD

A PLAN TO CHANGE YOUR LIFE

RAJAN ARYA

I would like to dedicate this book to my **Family**
For their continued
Support and Encouragements

Contents

FOREWORD

The book "**Roadmap To Study Abroad**" was developed to provide instructions on each and every move a student should take to enrol in an international university. Although I have made every attempt to make the information in this book as accurate as possible for all readers, data may occasionally alter or be updated by educational and governmental institutions.

I made an effort to make the book a practical guide and the go-to resource for learning all the ins and outs of studying abroad.

The book was written with the intention of advising and educating the reader about studying abroad. The information is not guaranteed to be accurate or comprehensive by the author, publisher, or publisher's affiliates. Both the author and the publisher are exempt from liability. The book was developed specifically to inform readers about studying abroad.

PREFACE

Before reading the book, I would like to share my general views on why you will choose to study abroad and the path you can choose to achieve your dream.

Studying abroad is a life-changing experience as you get the opportunity to kick start your future career. All the challenges you have faced throughout your academic life have all amounted to your progression to higher education.

For many students, including me, their college/university years are the most memorable and rewarding experience, and studying abroad makes that memory unforgettable for me also.

By studying abroad, you will get the chance to travel the globe, not only to the country you are studying. But you will find it easy to travel to other countries also. The question here arises: how?

There are specific courses and programs where students can access trips and excursions.

Certainly, living and studying abroad will help your personal development, as you will be learning and experiencing different cultures and lifestyles and thus enrich your perspective on life. You know all these factors hold the potential for creating unforgettable memories and allow you to incorporate them into your life. Your chances of gaining employment will increase, and that too at a perfect starting package.

Another important factor in studying abroad is the opportunity to learn a new language. Nowadays, the demand for bilingual workers is increasing with some employers, and even the employees offer language bonuses on your salary. Conversing in another language can help you connect with locals on their level, and you may even find yourself thinking or dreaming in their language. Learning a foreign language makes you smarter and improves your proficiency in your other tongue.

Remember: To have a second language is to have a second thought.

Studying abroad may allow you to save money, as many countries have low-cost living fees, which suit students that are on a tight budget. To surprise you, international tuition fees are cheaper as compared to universities in your home country.

You will also gain financial independence, and your confidence will increase as living in a foreign country away from family will give you a sense of independence that will boost your confidence and perspective on the world.

Global Times

Globalization is everywhere, and the professional world waits for you upon graduation. Technology keeps advancing, and employers seek workers having cross-cultural competence and cutting-edge technical skills.

As discussed, studying abroad expands your horizon while opening up a world of personal and professional opportunities. Globalization means wherever we live. We like to share our school communities, neighborhoods, clubs, and faiths with people of different backgrounds.

As a diver of career success, I feel that global experience is destined to continue moving from nice to must-have in today's marketplace.

You know... globalization is driving the demand for a U.S. workforce that possesses knowledge of other countries and cultures and is competent in languages other than English; most of the growth potential for the U.S. businesses lies in the overseas market, and the U.S. Department of state and defense have promoted and developed programs to encourage language learning and international study.

Understand study abroad enables today's students- the future leaders from all backgrounds and sectors- to gain access to international experiences that will help prepare them to be global citizens.

To meet the increasingly global marketplace demand upon graduation, studying abroad should be an essential component of many undergraduate degrees. Students need as much international exposure as they can get. Studying abroad is a smart way to establish your international credentials.

Since 2001, congress has helped address the disparity with the federally funded **Gilman International Scholarship Program, which** provides study abroad funds for low-income pell grant recipients.

Destinations for study abroad continue to expand and adapt to change in the global marketplace. With time study abroad programs will continue to change as the global economic and political landscape continue to evolve.

If you are looking for an opportunity to study abroad and then get into a job, I will advise you to consider studying in a rising global economy with strong GDP growth. Believe me, pushing yourself to get out of your comfort zone and experience another culture and education system in person is what makes studying abroad a meaningful and enlightening event, as it will become an integral part of your life.

While you are abroad, you will discover learning in a new way; you will experience a different approach to teaching, learning, assignments, and homework. Working with these differences will prepare you to work with colleagues, supervisors, and clients from diverse backgrounds.

After studying abroad, most students will never view their education in the same way again. The experience is so powerful that it often influences subsequent educational endeavors.

Remember:

- Be sure to connect the skills and the overall experience you gain during study abroad to your on-campus learning.
- Make sure the learned skills or characteristics can be applied in the workforce.
- Be prepared to appreciate and communicate your experience in a way your prospective employer will understand.

What value does studying abroad offer employers?

- Cross-cultural awareness.
- Ability to bring global thinking skills to bear on complex issues.
- Language skills are needed in a multilingual world.

Before going to read the book. Let's know the top **10 reasons to study abroad**:

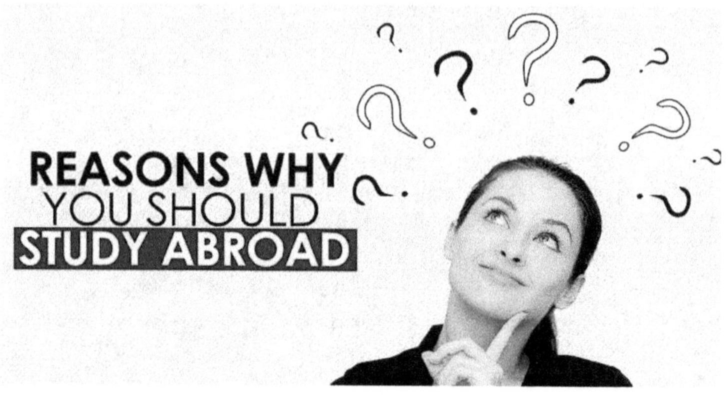

1. Learn about yourself and become self-aware.
2. Boost your self-confidence and independence.
3. Learn about our own country.
4. Learn another language.
5. The world view will expand.
6. Strengthen adaptability, communications, and team-building skills.
7. Enhance your career opportunities.
8. Experience another culture.
9. Travel.
10. Make new friends from around the world.

ACKNOWLEDGEMENTS

There are many people who have contributed to the publication of this book, and I would want to express my gratitude for their constant and unwavering support while I was writing it.

I want to thank my wife **Preeti Arya** and my son **Vedant Arya** first for inspiring me to write and for having the confidence to do it.

I want to thank my **mother** and **father** for being amazing people in my life. I want to thank everyone who has given me the chance to lead, follow, or collaborate with them for their mentorship and leadership.

Your contributions to my professional development and learning helped lay the groundwork for this book.

Prologue

The purpose of the book is to instruct readers on how to locate universities, compare them, and evaluate them in light of their preferences and needs. The topics covered in the book range from dreaming about studying abroad to selecting the best university and accommodations.

A checklist is provided at the end of the book and includes selecting the correct adviser, booking lodging, making sure your visa application is submitted on time, locating tickets, and learning about the customs and laws of other countries.

From the time you land in your ideal nation, the book will guide you through the steps you need to do.

This book will help you:

- Adapting to a new culture
- Concerning the four phases you could go through when you initially land in the host nation.
- Tips for achieving financial and academic success.

In order to help you decide which option is best for you, a list of all the options and possibilities will be presented to you at the end of this book.

I hope you enjoy it and make sure you understand everything since it will be very important to you in the future.

Wishing you luck
Rajan Arya

Rajan Arya

Rajan Arya is a famous entrepreneur and analytics expert. He was born in Kurukshetra, India, and was raised in Delhi. He is best known as the Co-founder of Infobirth Innovations, University Bureau, IELTS Bureau and Motor Tiger Inc.

From his childhood, Rajan Arya has been thinking about how to get into business and profit from it. He said

that he was on the quest for business ideas throughout his early childhood. He has been thinking about how to get into business and do something great for the society!

He was born to Indian parents. His father is a retired government officer, and his mother is a housewife. He is married to Preeti Arya, a national-level tennis player, and has a son Vedant Arya studying in class 1.

By the time he started working with:

- Investors Clinic Infratech Ltd as a Chief Digital Officer
- Armada Group (Kuwait) as Head of Digital
- Motion Infotech Pvt. Ltd. as Chief Digital Officer
- Rbs (Royal Bank Of Scotland) as Analyst Rmo
- Option Town Software's as Head Of Digital Marketing

Line which fully describes Rajan Arya as:

An Author, Blogger, and present Chief Digital Officer and Chief Executive Officer of Info Birth Innovations Pvt Ltd. & Info Birth Innovations INC, has experience of more than 13 years in delivering optimal results & business value via Data Science / Digital Marketing Solutions.

He conceptualized, developed, and led many new knowledge analytics-based capabilities which have had far- reaching industry impact.

He is passionate about Digital Marketing, Digital Transformation, Product Development /Marketing.

You can visit his website: Rajanarya.com, and reach to him on his linkedin account: https://www.linkedin.com/in/rajanaryaa/

ॐ

Why Study abroad?

Introduction

This book aims to educate students about study information abroad possibilities that will benefit their academic, social, and personal development.

Students will be immersed in a new culture through various programs ranging from semester experiences to short-term faculty programs while studying abroad.

When you study abroad, you can:

- Use most types of financial aid to cover program costs.
- Earn college credit.
- Learn a wide range of subjects in English.
- Expand your cultural horizons through exploring, discovering, and learning new things.

If you haven't already decided on a study abroad program, you may be unsure where to begin. Asking yourself the following questions is an excellent place to start:

- What do I want to learn while I'm overseas (a language? A specific field of study)?

- Do you wish to study abroad for a semester, a year, or only for the summer?
- Have I discussed how studying abroad would fit into my degree plan with my academic advisor?
- When looking at study abroad choices on our website, answering these questions for yourself might help you understand your objectives and reasons.

So let's explore the benefits and challenges of studying abroad.

Why to Study abroad?

Studying abroad is a life-changing experience and a great way to start your future career. You will get the chance to travel and live abroad. You will also learn and experience a different culture and lifestyle and enrich your perspective on life.

Studying abroad will increase your chances of gaining employment in a shorter period after graduation. Students worldwide travel across countries, continents, and oceans to acquire the best education available.

Figure 1.1: Why to study abroad

But why has it become so trendy to study at a university in another country?

Studying abroad offers several advantages, ranging from assisting you in finding a suitable job to boosting your social life. Still not convinced?

The following are the top eight reasons to study abroad.

1. **It's a difficult task:** It may seem weird to begin with this, but studying abroad is not always simple. Studying abroad has some unique obstacles,

but it is all part of the joy and experience. You may be concerned about leaving your nation, but don't be concerned; this is normal. One of the things that makes the experience so useful and meaningful is stepping outside of your comfort zone. After all, if you can study abroad, you can do anything!

2. **Learn about another culture:** For many international students, one of the most appealing aspects of studying abroad is the opportunity to immerse themselves in entirely other cultures. This enlightening journey will allow you to see and do things you would not anticipate and meet people from diverse cultures. For example, while living abroad, you'll have the opportunity to eat different foods, listen to traditional music, participate in local activities, and learn about all your host nation offers. It's also intriguing to experience your own culture through the eyes of another — you may learn a lot about yourself and your homeland this way!

3. **Excellent education:** Of course, your ultimate objective will always be to obtain the best possible education no matter where you study. Being an international student might considerably expand your educational opportunities. After all, why restrict yourself to universities in your own country? Often, studying at a foreign institution is the best option for you. For example, the United States, the United Kingdom, and Australia all have highly respected higher education institutions, and these three nations are home to a large share of the world's top universities.

4. **Opportunity to learn a new language:** One of the most significant advantages of studying abroad is learning a new language. Learning a language might be difficult, but nothing compares to living in a country where the language is spoken natively. It is pretty beneficial! Because English is widely spoken, studying in the United States or the United Kingdom may be pretty beneficial. You'll be able to learn in English, converse with locals, and improve your language abilities.

5. **Possibilities for employment:** Of course, the primary motivation for pursuing a degree is to advance your professional opportunities. Employers increasingly value graduates with foreign experience and education in today's globalized, well-connected society. Learning new languages, appreciating different cultures, overcoming the hardships of living in another country, and broadening your worldview benefit from studying abroad. All of these qualities are sought by modern firms when recruiting, and they will only grow in importance in the future.

6. **Meet new people**: Whichever university you attend, you'll meet many new people and develop new friends who are in the same boat as you. Studying abroad gives you a once-in-a-lifetime opportunity to meet individuals from various walks of life and learn about other nations and cultures. Many lifelong connections begin at university, and you'll have the opportunity to live, learn, and travel with them while you're there. Knowing people from different nations worldwide may also be advantageous, especially after you graduate!

7. **Traveling internationally**: You will be able to go to other surrounding countries and experience the culture of your study place. For example, if you attend a UK institution, you may quickly fly to continental Europe to see Paris, Rome, Barcelona, and other great cities. Studying abroad provides a once-in-a-lifetime opportunity to travel the world while also providing a satisfying educational experience. Seeing various regions of the world will undoubtedly shape your character and outlook and prepare you for life in a global society.

8. **Become self-sufficient**: Going to university is typically described as the point at which you become independent of your parents and relatives. This is especially true if you attend university in a foreign nation. To complete the circle, being self-sufficient is a task in and of itself. However, living and studying in a different nation will help you grow into a self-reliant and adventurous adult prepared to excel in your future job.

The benefits of studying abroad

Studying abroad may be one of the most rewarding experiences for a college student. Students can study in a distant country and experience the charm and culture of a different culture by studying abroad.

Figure 1.2: Benefits of studying abroad

The top ten benefits of studying abroad are listed below:

1. **Explore the World**: The opportunity to travel the world is the most compelling incentive to pursue a study abroad program. By studying abroad, you will have the opportunity to go to a new nation and explore different cultures, customs, and activities. One advantage of studying abroad is the ability to experience different terrains, natural marvels, museums, and landmarks in your host country. Furthermore, you will not be confined to visiting only the country where you are studying; you will also be able to visit adjacent countries! If you study in France, for example, you will have the opportunity to travel around Europe, including London, Barcelona, and Rome.

2. **Education:** Another reason you could consider studying abroad is to gain exposure to diverse educational approaches. Enrolling in a study abroad program will allow you to experience a side of your major that you would not have had access to at home. You'll discover that fully immersing yourself in your host country's educational system is a fantastic opportunity to truly experience and appreciate the people, customs, and culture. Education is at the heart of every study abroad trip—after all, it is a study abroad program—and picking the appropriate institution is crucial.

3. **Incorporate a New Culture**: Many students who opt to study abroad make their first trip outside their native country. The different cultural viewpoints intrigue them when they arrive in their new host nation.

You will discover fantastic fresh meals, customs, traditions, and social environments while studying abroad. You will have a deeper knowledge and appreciation for the people and history of the United States. You will be able to observe an entirely different way of living.

4. **Improve Your Language Abilities**: If you're considering studying abroad, you're probably interested in learning a foreign language. Studying abroad allows you to immerse yourself entirely in a new language, and there is no better way to learn than to get straight in. In addition to the extensive language practice you will receive daily; your host university will most likely offer language classes to supplement your academic study. Immerse yourself in a new culture and expand your horizons beyond the classroom.

5. **Possibilities for Employment:** When you return home after your study abroad program, you will have a new perspective on culture, language skills, a superb education, and a desire to learn. All of them are, without a doubt, incredibly appealing to potential employers. Many students fall in love with their host nation and opt to stay and work there. If you can relate, you will discover that obtaining a local education will be quite beneficial when looking for a career in that nation.

6. **Discover New Interests**: If you're still not convinced, consider this: studying in a different nation exposes you to various new hobbies and interests that you would not have found otherwise. You may learn that you have an unknown knack for hiking, water sports, snow skiing, golf, or a variety of other new sports that you have never attempted at home. You'll also get to try out some new and intriguing entertainment options. You may enjoy plays, movies, dancing, nightclubs, and concerts, to name a few things.

7. **Make Friends Forever:** One of the most valuable aspects of studying abroad is the ability to make new acquaintances from all walks of life. You will attend school and live among students from your host nation while studying abroad. This allows you to get to know your classmates better and form lasting bonds with them. Attempt to keep in touch with your overseas pals once your study abroad program has ended. These buddies can be valuable networking tools in the future, in addition to satisfying personal ties.

8. **Personal Improvement:** There's nothing quite like being alone in a strange land. You could discover that studying abroad brings out your natural independence. Students who study abroad become explorers of

their new country, revealing their natural curiosity and excitement. One advantage of studying abroad is exploring oneself while learning about a foreign culture. Being alone in a new area can be intimidating at times, and it puts your capacity to adjust to various settings while also solving problems to the test.

9. **Admissions to Graduate School**: Graduate school admissions committees, like potential employers, highly value study abroad experiences. Students who study abroad demonstrate their variety by taking on new tasks and putting themselves in challenging situations. Most essential, students who have studied abroad demonstrate their dedication to their studies. Graduate schools are always looking for people who will add something special to their institution. Students who have studied abroad have demonstrated that they possess the curiosity and educational aptitude necessary to succeed in graduate school.

10. **Experiential Learning**: What are the benefits of studying abroad? For most students, this may be their last chance to go overseas for an extended time. You will eventually find work and a profession, and studying abroad may be a once-in-a-lifetime chance. Take advantage of this chance to explore the world without obligations other than studying and learning about different cultures. Studying abroad is a once-in-a-lifetime opportunity.

The challenges of studying abroad

Studying abroad has its advantages, but it also has its drawbacks. Homesickness from being too far away from family, course requirements of existing curriculum, finances, language, cultural challenges, and health and food issues are significant concerns when studying abroad. While some of these problems are unavoidable, international students must understand more to better prepare for them.

Figure 1.3: Challenges of studying abroad

1. **Homesickness:** Students who had previously studied abroad were more likely to experience homesickness, with many confessing having difficulty adjusting to living alone in a strange country. The lack of a readily available support system, such as a close relative, commonly impacts first-time study abroad students. While studying abroad, 92 percent say they miss the familiarities of home, with 57 percent stating it is the sensory experience they miss the most, and 74 percent saying they miss the noises of their hometown. Overall, 99 percent of international students said their decision to study abroad was good. However, adapting to new surroundings proved to be a challenge. At least once a week, 43% of respondents said they were homesick. Furthermore, 49% feel that being away from family and friends hindered their academic performance, and 40% believe homesickness impaired their sleep. The poll also discovered that the highest sensations of homesickness occur late at night, between 10 p.m. and 12 a.m.

2. **Existing curriculum course requirements**: Some students consider studying abroad a stumbling block in their academic advancement. Adolescents who have previously set the quickest route to graduate from their chosen major are frequently affected. The fear of delaying their development by spending a semester or more abroad is a motivation for rejecting study abroad possibilities to go overseas. Furthermore, students are concerned about being forced to study courses that may or may not

apply to their courses.

3. **Cultural and Language barriers**: International students, especially in their initial few months, confront a variety of academic issues as well as cultural and language challenges. Academics, in particular, are doomed unless pupils overcome language and cultural barriers. Additional language classes are routinely provided to international students who are not skilled in English, although the format of these lessons is generally not tailored to meet academic standards. In a poll of overseas students in the United Kingdom, half said they had trouble reaching the requisite level of English to follow their courses. Meanwhile, 43 percent of students stated that language hurdles impacted their overall education and grades, and 30 percent had to move from their significant courses to English language classes. Cultural barriers also negatively influence pupils' academic and language development. According to the same poll, 17 percent of students stated cultural differences had little impact on their education, while 40% indicated cultural differences have a significant impact.

4. **Financial difficulties**: Studying abroad may be quite expensive. Unless they come from wealthy families, international students frequently suffer financial hardships during their studies. Understandably, tuition prices are substantially more for them than for local courses. Adapting to a host nation, such as managing everyday activities and engaging in local cultural events, may need additional costs in addition to academic obligations. The extra money may be difficult because international students on tight study-only visas are typically not permitted to work outside of the university. This might be one of the top adjustment challenges for study abroad students is a lack of financial resources.

5. **Health and dietary concerns**: International students, like housing, have a strong emotional need for both filling and familiar cuisine. Educators have recognized the relevance of good, familiar meals in a visiting student's entire experience. Several students mentioned food insecurity, which may be characterized as a temporary or persistent inability to acquire nutritious and desirable meals that allow one to live a functioning life, was mentioned by several students. Students expressed melancholy, loneliness, identity loss, hunger, weight loss or gain challenges, and accounts of being compelled to sacrifice religious convictions to eat."

Case study

Do you intend to continue your education after completing 12th grade in your native country? Are you stumped as to where to begin? You are not alone, so don't worry. Many students worldwide opt to study in a new setting and environment to have a unique experience. There are other possibilities available to you worldwide, not just 1 or 2.

After 12th grade, consider studying overseas.

After finishing 12th grade, you can pursue an undergraduate degree and study abroad.

Studying abroad for an undergraduate degree provides you with the following benefits:

- Intercultural communication skills
- Language skills
- Leadership abilities
- Independent management
- A high level of maturity to survive in a new environment

All of these abilities provide you with a competitive advantage in the job market and may benefit any company in today's global economy.

What is the best way to study abroad after 12th grade?

Getting into overseas universities is not challenging. You only need to follow a simple procedure to get to your desired location. There are just six stages to studying abroad after 12th grade. Here you can find thorough information on how you may study abroad after finishing 12th grade.

1. **Identify the field to study abroad:** At an international institute, you have a variety of possibilities to choose from. However, you must select the appropriate course that best matches your abilities and interests.

2. **Identify the study abroad destination**: Choosing the nation where you want to continue your education after high school is critical. Factors that should be considered primarily are Climate, Culture, Language, Cost of study, Cost and standard of living, Research opportunities, Internships opportunities.

3. **Identify the universities to study abroad:** After deciding on an area of study and a place, the next step is to choose which universities to attend. This selection must be based on academic and research prospects in your field of study's department and available courses and prices. Take notice of the application deadline as well as the qualifications.

4. **Take the standardized tests to study abroad**: You should take the standardized examinations that would qualify you for admission based on the prerequisites of the courses you want to attend. The prerequisites for tests and results vary depending on your chosen courses and universities. Here is a short list of foreign tests that are frequently asked: a. English language proficiency examinations include IELTS, TOEFL, Duolingo, or PTE; other language competency tests include French, German, and Chinese, among others. B. Tests such as the SAT or ACT will assess your verbal, quantitative, reasoning, and topic knowledge.

5. **Apply to the universities to study abroad**: The deadline for applying to institutions should be adhered to. You will need to provide specific supporting papers and the completed application form. The documents required are Mark sheets, Transcripts, Score reports for the tests, Financial capability certificate, Statement of Purpose, Letter of Recommendation, Application Essays. If your qualifications meet the standards for admission to foreign colleges after 12th grade, submit all essential papers carefully to receive a favorable response.

6. **Apply for the required Student visa**: After verifying your acceptance, the next step is applying for a student visa. A valid student visa is required to visit any new nation to take lessons. You can apply online, at a nearby embassy, or through a consultant. To apply, fill out the application form and send it with the relevant documentation. The list of commonly requested documents are Filled visa application form, A Valid Passport, Proof of a Bonafide Student, Financial evidence of enough funds to study and stay abroad, Scores of Language Proficiency, Admission letter in the abroad university, Transcripts of previous education (if required)

7. **Best courses to study abroad after 12th**: If you plan to study in a foreign university after graduating high school, carefully select your subject and

course. After the 12th grade, I have listed overseas methods in each subject of study.

Study abroad after 12th commerce

After finishing your 12th grade, you will have a wide range of options for studying abroad in the subject of commerce.

After 12th commerce, the most popular courses to study abroad are:

- Bachelor of Business Administration
- Diploma in Business Administration
- B.S. in Management Science
- BA in Management Science
- BA in Finance Management
- BA in Accounting Management
- B.Com. (Finance and Accounting)
- Marketing
- Economics
- Mathematics

Australia, Canada, the UK, Germany, and Singapore are some countries with commerce-related colleges such as Victoria University, University of Toronto, Munich Business school, etc.

Study abroad after 12th Science

Students in the scientific discipline might select between a medical or non-medical track. In both ways, you can take courses to study abroad. Choose a stream based on your interests.

Some of the greatest scientific methods for studying abroad after 12th grade are listed below:

- Study abroad after 12th medical
- Doctor (MBBS)
- Veterinary (B.V.Sc)
- Homeopathy (BHMS)
- Ayurveda (BAMS)

- Optometry (B.Optom.)
- Public Health Administration
- Occupational Therapy
- Physiotherapy
- Clinical Research
- Radiology
- Audiology

The UK, the USA, Canada, and Australia have the best colleges that specialize in medical courses.

Study abroad after 12th Non Medical

After 12th grade, you can study engineering in another country if you pick a non-medical field. The following are some of the most popular non-medical courses:

- Chemistry
- B.S. in Engineering Management
- Bachelor of Engineering Management
- Mechanical Engineering
- Civil Engineering
- Electrical Engineering
- IT Engineering
- Biomedical Engineering
- Energy Management and Engineering
- Aeronautical Engineering
- Automobile Engineering
- Sound Engineering
- Civil engineering

These are the best courses to study after the 12th science group. The USA, Australia, the UK, Singapore, and Germany are some of the best countries to study engineering.

Study abroad after 12th arts

You can select the arts field if you are not interested in commerce or science. After finishing your 12th grade, there is no doubt that you will be able to discover art courses all around the world. The following are some of the most popular courses:

- Bachelor of Arts (B.A)
- Journalism and Mass Communications
- Law
- Bachelor of Business Administration (B.B.A.)
- Fine Arts
- Hotel Management
- B.S. in Product Design
- Bachelor of Interior Design
- BA in Interior Design

The arts stream helps the students in verbal and written communication. The countries that offer the best education in the arts stream are the UK, France, the USA, and Canada.

Study abroad after 12th with a scholarship

You can apply for scholarships if you can't afford to pay for your study abroad expenditures. International students can apply for a variety of scholarships all across the world. Governments and colleges in other countries will offer you scholarships to study overseas after 12th grade.

To be eligible for a scholarship to study abroad after 12th grade, you must have certain unique qualities, like as:

- an excellent academic record,
- good skills-set,
- excellence in sports or other activities etc.

Scholarships for Undergraduate Students in Foreign Universities

For Indian students, there are various places where they may study abroad at a reasonable cost. You have the option of selecting one of them. However, if you wish to study in one of the more expensive first-world nations, don't worry about the expense. International students who want to study in another country can apply for various scholarships.

Many prestigious colleges provide substantial scholarship opportunities. Scholarships are one of the most acceptable methods to lower your costs when studying abroad. There are merit-based scholarships, need-based scholarships, and other types of scholarships.

These are the scholarships that you can apply to study abroad:

- TATA Scholarships
- Inlaks Scholarships
- Ritchie-Jennings Memorial Scholarship
- Shastri Indo-Canadian Fellowships
- The Oxford and Cambridge Society of India Scholarship
- Leverage Edu Scholarship
- JN Tata Endowment Scholarship
- National Scholarship Programme of the Slovak Republic
- MEXT Scholarship for Japan
- Rutherford International Fellowship Program
- Erasmus scholarship
- Chevening Scholarship
- Scholarships in the USA
- Fulbright Scholarship
- Yale Silver Scholar Program
- Inlaks Shivdasani Foundation Scholarship
- Gates Millennium Scholarship
- Harvard Scholarship
- Ratan Tata Scholarship for Engineering Students
- AICPA John L. Carey Scholarship Award
- Stanford Reliance Dhirubhai Fellowships for Indian Students
- The Hubert H. Humphrey Fellowship Programme
- The Indian Trust Fellowship
- American University Emerging Global Leader Scholarship
- Tata Scholarships for Cornell University

Scholarships in Canada

- Shastri Indo-Canadian Fellowships
- President Scholarship in Canada
- Vanier Canada Graduate Scholarships
- University of Waterloo International Master's and Doctoral Awards

- Ontario Graduate Scholarship
- University of Manitoba Graduate Fellowship
- University of Calgary Graduate Awards and Scholarships
- Ontario Trillium Scholarship
- UBC Graduate Global Leadership Fellowships
- Trudeau Foundation Scholarships

Scholarships in Australia

- Undergraduate Academic Excellence International Scholarship in Australia
- UNSW International Scholarships
- Dr. Abdul Kalam International Postgraduate Scholarship
- Charles Darwin University Vice-Chancellor's International High Achievers Scholarships
- Flinders International Postgraduate Scholarships
- Adelaide Global Excellence Scholarships for International Students

Scholarships in New Zealand

- New Zealand Commonwealth Scholarships 2022
- New Zealand International Doctoral Research Scholarships (NZIDRS)
- Victoria Master's Scholarship
- A-C Rayner Memorial Scholarship
- SEG Scholarship
- The Eamon Molloy Memorial Scholarship

Popular countries to study abroad after 12th

Several places throughout the world provide outstanding education and the opportunity to work and study. Most Indian students studying abroad choose nations such as the United States, the United Kingdom, Canada, Australia, and Germany since they are among the greatest places to study abroad.

- **Canada**: For Indian students, Canada is the most popular study abroad location. Diplomas, Associate's, Bachelor's, Master's degrees, and more degrees can be obtained by studying in Canada. Canadian universities are committed to research and quality teaching, allowing their students to adapt to any type of school or work environment worldwide.

- **USA:** Studying in the United States has become popular among Indian youngsters. The United States has the most significant number of international students. The country offers associate, bachelor's, master's, and other degrees. The university and the course itself determine the length of each course.
- **UK:** Higher education in the United Kingdom is often regarded as the greatest in the world. More than 55,000 Indian students study in the UK, making it the country with the most Indian students. Some of the intriguing learning techniques used in the nation include lectures, seminars, tutorials, and workshops.
- **Australia:** Australia has the most universities listed among the top 100 institutions in the world. More than 20,000 programs are available in the country's colleges. Bachelor's, master's, and doctoral degrees are the three levels of higher education. Universities use research-based learning in the classroom to apply concepts.
- **Germany:** Studying in Germany is an excellent option for an Indian student who wants to study abroad. Management and applied science courses are well-known in the nation. Germany is famed for its car sector, and many colleges in the country provide job opportunities when students complete their studies.
- **New Zealand:** The UK education system, which uses research-based teaching, has affected New Zealand's educational system. New Zealand colleges provide courses ranging from vocational to Ph.D. levels. New Zealand graduates are in great demand due to a skills deficit in the country.
- **France:** For Indian students, France is the finest destination to study abroad. The French government provides financial assistance to students, and the French language is included in the curriculum. After graduation, colleges in France give a variety of career prospects.
- **Singapore:** Singapore is home to more than 15 of the world's top institutions, which provide world-class education and research opportunities. Singapore is also one of the most affordable destinations for international students. Because of the open business culture and constant development, there are more job opportunities after graduation.

Take Expert Help

Studying abroad is one of the most challenging and life-changing decisions. As a result, the processes that must be followed are not simple. In that circumstances, consulting study abroad specialists is the most effective strategy to realize your dreams. To make this dream come true, I have made a platform University Bureau.

It explains how to make study abroad students' dreams come true. In this industry, we have over 20 years of expertise. We can assist you in locating the courses you wish to study at the best institution or college for you.

We work with over 1500+ famous institutions, schools, and colleges across Australia, Canada, the United Kingdom, and the United States. More than 50,000 students have benefitted from our services and were accepted into prestigious colleges across Canada, the United States, the United Kingdom, and Australia.

We're confident that, with access to a database containing a variety of courses and programs, we'll be able to aid you in determining what's best for you.

We make every effort to ensure that all students are informed of each phase of the international admissions process. We make you surpass your expectations in all the entrance exams such as TOEFL, IELTS, GMAT, GRE, and SAT, which are needed for overseas admissions.

In addition, the University Bureau team is in charge of all visa documents and interview preparation procedures. Our entire faculty is up to date and experience. The staff analyzes every student's profile and is guided through the procedure.

I will share the details about the platform in the coming chapters.

There are various career-enhancing benefits of studying abroad. Studying abroad is the first step in a profession that will lead to a smooth transition in your life.

Studying abroad provides you with certifications that are recognized all around the world. The essential duty is to concentrate on the standardized examinations and language competence assessments necessary for admittance to overseas universities.

Preparing for and passing examinations such as the TOEFL, IELTS, GMAT, GRE, and SAT, as well as having a strong educational background, will help you advance.

Additionally, working with a company specializing in studying abroad might make the process go more smoothly. An education consulting firm can provide comprehensive services and assist you in acing all of your examinations for international admissions.

Courses should be adequately shortlisted, and the application process should be managed with care. Studying abroad is not for the faint of heart!

You may confront various challenges, such as a language barrier, currency variations, changes in teaching styles, homesickness, and so on, but the experience you receive will enable you to adapt to and conquer all of life's challenges.

By this, I hope you have understood the challenges, benefits, and, most notably, the first step to study abroad.

We shall discuss in detail the next step in the coming chapters and share my personal experience to boost your confidence.

------*****---------

II

Your first step

There are many perks of studying abroad, being prepared and organized will help you and ease your transition from home to chosen destination. Applying to a university, transitioning and moving can be fast and easy if dealt successfully. Adapting and becoming familiar with the new culture, location and language may be hard but never let this discourage you.

Most obvious challenge which you may face with studying abroad is the "language barrier", as you need a short time to learn language, phrases and vocabular which the locals use and you will get comfortable with it once you begin interacting and adapting to the new lifestyle.

At the start of your journey it may be confusing about the currency, but by using the correct currency and a reliable conversion system it will be beneficial and help you in adapting and avoiding financial problems.

Figure 2.1: Your first step to study abroad

Also, cultural differences an range from anything to customary handshakes whilst greeting people to other social norms. Apart from researching the countries cultural elements, seeing and copying what others do is may be beneficial.

Even if you have set a clear goal that you want to attend a certain university it is wise and best to apply at different universities that offer the same department you wish to study.

With this, choosing the right country to study is also essential, as financial options offered by countries are different and loan, grants and scholarship vary according to departments and universities. Finding a university is accredited and has your desired department is crucial for being successful in your future academic career.

Residency and travel visas also vary from country to country. So, it is important to find out about all the laws and restrictions of the country you are considering to studying in.

Before choosing the department of studying, think about your passion, identify your interest. **Some helpful questions you may ask yourself are:**

- What is your priority?
- Which majors have the most earning power?
- Which careers pay the best salaries?
- Which profession best matches your personality?
- Which majors are most in demand?

You also need to choose your accommodation, for which you need to consider:

- Length/duration of your program
- Your financial budget
- Location
- Choosing a house/roommate
- Check before you arrive

So, by now, you have understood that the studying abroad is a serious undertaking as it will challenge you on a personal level, impact your academic career, and cost money.

The following statements, give you an honest "thumbs up" or "thumbs down" on whether you agree with the following statements:

1. I thrive on challenges- the more the better.
2. I enjoy meeting and getting to know new people.
3. I love new places, new food and new culture.
4. I can get along with many different personalities.
5. I thrive on change and I am happy to be surrounded b it 24x7.
6. I enjoy taking calculated risks.
7. I don't get bothered by things that seem different or strange.
8. I don't mind being alone.
9. I go to the extra mile time and again without being asked.
10. I am adaptable.
11. I am a good listener and communicator.
12. Can handle failure and learn from it.

Scoring:

- If you answered yes to 10 out of 12, you will have a bright global future.
- If you answered yes to 8 out of 12, you will be a good internationalist.
- If you said yes to half, you should think seriously about the kind of study abroad program will best meet your needs and help out to evolve.
- If you said yes to less than five, you should consider why you want to study abroad and do a little preparation.

So before, studying abroad consider yourself to answer the following questions:

1. What do you want to study?
2. How important is it that you earn credit for studying abroad?
3. Where do you want to study and why?
4. Where and with whom do you want to live?
5. How long do you want to be overseas?
6. How proficient are you in a second language?
7. What is the program going to cost?
8. Are you constantly receiving financial aids?
9. Do you have a job or internship that will be adversely affected?
10. How much freedom do you want or need?

11. What do you want most out of the experience?

The questions above asked, will help you begin to sort through the many considerations, you will need to weigh about any individual program. But keep in mind that although these practical elements are all important to some degree or another. An open mind and your level of personal preparedness will probably have the greatest impact on your international experience.

Now, let's discuss about the credit system:

Every college and university set its own guideline regarding how it approves study abroad coursework. There are two standard types of credit:

1. **Resident credit:** It's an extension of your studies on the home campus. Your study abroad grades will be calculated into your overall GPA and individual courses will appear on your transcript.
2. **Transfer credit:** Treats you as a student who has taken a leave of absence. You will need to request an official transcript form the accredited U.S. or foreign institution with an English translation.

Always remember that proper planning and preparation enhances your success to study abroad.

Top 10 tips for deciding to study abroad:

1. Make sure you are ready for the personal challenges.
2. Determine how studying abroad will enhance your degree.
3. Crunch the number to conform you have the necessary funds.
4. Choose a place that you are particularly interested in or curious about.
5. Consider the important role of language learning abroad.
6. Confirm that your credits can be transferred.
7. Know that you will benefit ore if you don't hang out primarily with others.
8. Articulate your personal goals for studying abroad.
9. Talk with professors, friends, parents about the opportunity.
10. Prepare properly to enhance your success abroad.

Introduction

Choosing to study abroad is an excellent first step on your path to higher education. International study may be beneficial to your future since it allows you to learn about various cultures, meet new people, have access to a larger selection of educational institutions, and add to your CV/resume, which may help you find work. It may, however, be a difficult decision. Where should I go to school? Is it something I can afford? How do I submit my application? All of these and other questions are common, and there are people who can assist you find answers!

You may have a general notion of what you want to learn about studying abroad, but if you're not sure where to begin, consider the following:

- Which country should I study in and why – which country do you believe would best fit your needs? Consider the expense of school and living, as well as the country's educational quality and proximity to your family and friends. Do you want to stay close to home or move further away for adventure?
- What should I study abroad and why - what is your existing academic background, and do you match the general entrance requirements? Have you considered what sort of job you'd like to pursue and what kind of course might be appropriate? For how long do you intend to study? Some nations offer four-year courses that are equal to three years in another country.
- When do you wish to begin your studies, and how much time do you have left in school? How long will it take for my application to be reviewed and accepted? Have you taken into account the time it will take to gather paperwork and apply for a visa, if one is required?

Figure 2.2: Studying abroad

- What does it cost to study abroad - this includes more than just tuition fees? As examples, application costs, visa fees, lodging and living expenditures, health insurance, and entertainment must all be considered.
- What will I do to pay for my overseas study - are you a great candidate for a scholarship? Is there any financial assistance or bursaries available from your government? Is this a financially viable option for your family, either on its own or with a student loan?
- There are numerous stages you may take before deciding where you wish to study throughout the world. Let's discuss some useful hints that will perhaps help you get started and feel more confidence in your decision.

Your ultimate career plans

Thank you for making the decision to study abroad. Perhaps you're going to Italy for a fashion design summer course, the United Kingdom for an MA in political science, or Amsterdam for a semester of engineering. Your thoughts are most likely filled with excitement and expectation as you prepare to travel—new people, languages, meals, lifestyle, culture, weather, and travel. While all of these new experiences may be intimidating, you understand the importance of travelling overseas. You'll not only have a nice time, but you'll also get foreign experience that will improve your work opportunities in the future.

Consider adding another layer to your experience to better prepare for today's competitive job market: boost your time abroad by adding career-enhancing professional experiences. Careers are formed over time, and you can add value to your time overseas by doing a few extra things that will look good on your resume and demonstrate to foreign employers that you understand the global workplace. Here are a few pointers to help you get the most out of your study abroad experience in terms of "career punch."

Figure 2.3: Career plan to study abroad

Establish your career objectives

- The modern global economy requires foreign experience as part of our education, and studying abroad is a great way to get these credentials. Before you leave home, you should start thinking about your future career. Here are some objectives to keep in mind as you prepare for your trip.
- A major goal should be to get professional experience. If you don't leave home with this goal in mind, you'll likely get caught up in the excitement of being overseas and overlook the fact that you're missing out on a fantastic opportunity to obtain professional foreign experience. Before you go, the first step is to update your résumé.

Figure 2.4: Career objectves to study abroad

- Make the most of your study abroad experience by developing cross-cultural skills. Future employers, particularly foreign ones, will value your personality over your academic credentials (although these are also important). People who thrive internationally have a special combination of abilities and traits—a high international IQ, according to international recruiters. You should take use of your time overseas to mix and mingle with individuals from different cultures, including "professional" mixing and mingling.
- While studying abroad, don't exclusively concentrate on your studies. The quantity of classes you take while overseas will not impress future employers, and they may not even look at your grades. Your ability to integrate into a new workplace will pique an employer's attention.
- Demonstrate initiative across cultures. Take the initiative to do a few career-building tasks while overseas to demonstrate your worth to potential employers. Organize an event, volunteer in your industry, or schedule a meeting with experts in your field. These tiny efforts will demonstrate to potential employers that you have what it takes to thrive in a new culture, and if you can show several examples of initiative in a culture different than your own, your future CV will shine brighter.

Develop your professional skills

- While studying abroad, there are several opportunities to expand your professional skills. Even brief professional encounters will add to your resume's value.
- Become a member of a multicultural student work group. Look for classes that demand group work and will allow you to obtain useful cross-cultural experience. (Wording on resume: "Always sought out courses that required teamwork with students from many cultures. I learned to appreciate the multicultural workplace where my culture was in the minority ")

Figure 2.5: Develop your professional skills

- As a researcher, intern or volunteer with a well-known professor in your subject. Professors find it difficult to employ international students, so offer your talents instead. If all else fails, find a local graduate student who is conducting research and offer to help with him or her on a voluntary basis. Because your time abroad is generally limited, start using these tactics as soon as you get on campus.
- Make your English skills available in nations where English is not the primary language. You may easily put your English language abilities to use by assisting a professor with the editing of a paper for an international conference, teaching English to fellow students, or

assisting an organization with the development of an English-language website. Consider compiling a dictionary of English terminology relevant to your field of study and teaching a course on these terms to your classmates. There are several ways to share your English language talents.

- While travelling abroad, network with experts in your field. Imagine leading a small group of international engineering students in organizing a visit to a local research and development engineering business in your field. This approach is simple to implement. Alternatively, if you are a political science student, you may plan a visit to an international organization's headquarters in a nearby city to speak with specialists. Alternatively, you may prepare an essay for one of your classes that requires you to meet local experts in your subject. This is a fantastic networking opportunity that you can even put on your resume.
- Off campus, preferably in your profession, volunteer. Extend your international living experience beyond the academic setting by learning about the local community.
- Extend your stay in another country. Include a one-month internship, a language course, or professional cross-cultural travel. A professional internship can increase the value of your study abroad experience on your CV for the expense of an extra month.
- Outside the Classroom, Gain Cross-Cultural Experience
- Professionalize your experience to demonstrate to employers that you are familiar with other cultures.
- Be wary of the ghetto for international students. You will lose out on a lot of cross-cultural learning if you simply hang out with kids from your native country.
- Join student groups with a majority of local students. Your goal is to meet local acquaintances and maybe join one of their initiatives as a leader.
- Learn how to properly explain the culture of your host nation. When explaining another culture, it's simple to be professional. Read a few books about your host country's cultural past. You can then impress possible employers by writing a short professional overview of your host country's cultural standards.
- Connect with local families and explore the area. Make friends with the students and their families. These visits give useful information that may be included in a resume later.

- Learn the language of the area. Any worldwide profession requires language acquisition. Even acquiring a simple vocabulary will help you solidify ties and show potential employers that you are interested in languages.

Choose the right program

Studying abroad is an amazing chance for students to travel the world. However, sorting between the hundreds of places and program that all seem appealing may be difficult. This guide will assist you in narrowing down your options so that you may choose the best study abroad program for you.

Selecting a study abroad program might be difficult. We've all heard how "studying abroad will alter your life," and although there's plenty to be enthusiastic about, there's also the dread of making a mistake.

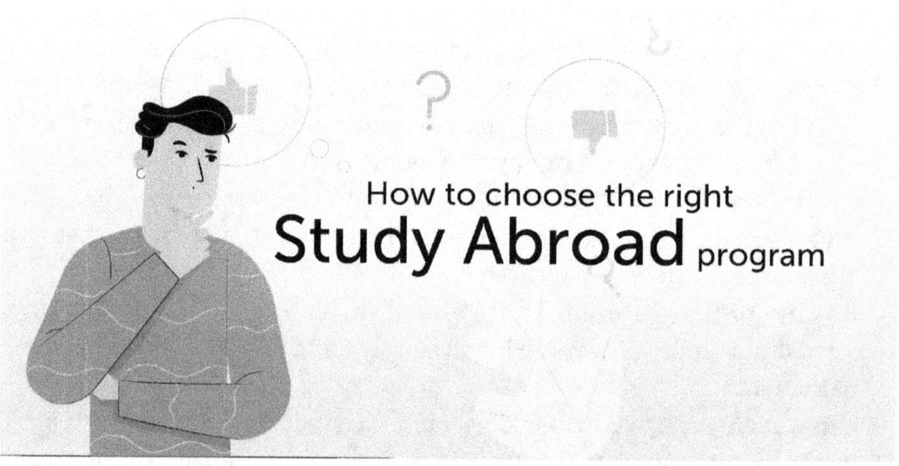

Figure 2.6: Choose the right program

I got it. For years, I'd envisioned studying abroad as an integral part of my college education. The trouble was that the details altered with each fantasy! I fantasized of learning French in southern France at times. At other times, I fantasized about spending a semester at sea. I felt a lot of pressure to pick the "right" study abroad program since I knew it would have a lasting influence on my life.

If you're anything like me, you're a freshman or sophomore in college with no idea where to begin when it comes to selecting a study abroad program. Fortunately, the methods outlined below should assist you in making an informed decision.

Choosing a study abroad program

When it comes to selecting a study abroad program, there is no one-size-fits-all solution. Here are some things to think about to help you narrow down the finest program for you.

1. **Choose the country where you want to study:** The initial step may appear to be the most difficult. You must first decide where you wish to study abroad. It's fine if narrowing things down to a certain country feels too challenging. Consider an area or a shared characteristic (such as language) that binds a group of countries together. Looking at language requirements is the quickest approach to limit down your options. Many studies abroad program involve lessons conducted at a local institution, necessitating the knowledge of the local language. If you speak a foreign language well, you might feel more at ease looking for program where you'll be directly enrolled in a local institution. Don't worry if you don't speak a language other than English. You may study abroad in English-speaking nations such as England, South Africa, Australia, New Zealand, and others by enrolling directly in local universities. Furthermore, several other nations, such as Denmark, Sweden, and Germany, have substantial English-language program. Due to the way the program is operated, there are also many programs that do not have a language requirement. These programs are usually provided by a third party (like IELTS Bureau). Because these programs are aimed at foreign students, they tend to include more English programs in countries where English is not the first language. If you're on the other end of the spectrum and haven't yet decided where you want to study abroad, now is the time to be inspired. Examine study abroad Instagram profiles and the pamphlets in your college's study abroad office.

2. **Examine programs that apply to your major:** There are many different types of study abroad programs available, ranging from month-long language exchanges to year-long programs and even online study abroad programs. Try to narrow your search to programs that are relevant to

your major. The good news is that there is study abroad opportunities for almost every major! You can look at study abroad opportunities for business majors, education majors, fashion majors, and a variety of other majors. Pre-medical study abroad programs, as well as programs in a variety of other majors, are available. You may also seek guidance from your home institution's study abroad office if you wish to delve beyond an internet search. Your department chair is also a good source of information on the appropriate program for your major. Also, you are not need to study abroad in the same department as your major! A semester study abroad in a region you're interested in can be a terrific way to broaden your horizons and make your college experience more well-rounded.

3. **Determine the length of your study abroad program:** After you've reduced your search to a few locations or programs, you'll need to decide how long you want to spend studying abroad. Study abroad programs, as you may know, come in a variety of forms and sizes, ranging from a few weeks to a whole year.

4. **Look into financial aid options:** The next step is a very practical one: financial assistance! Study abroad programs can be as cheap as your home institution's tuition or as expensive as your home institution's tuition. If the cost of the program you've chosen is exorbitant, there are many of opportunities for study abroad financial help. Your initial point of contact should be your chosen study abroad program; many programs provide specific scholarships for students each semester. Send an email to the program leader and ask for advice. It's also a good idea to seek for scholarships from organizations that aren't affiliated with your program.

5. **Read testimonials and speak with former study abroad students:** You've probably limited down your alternatives greatly by this point. However, you're probably still divided between a few options. I propose that you read internet evaluations of the study abroad program you're considering. You may look up your software and read a lot of reviews, and you can even narrow down to the most current ones. Simply reading a few reviews can reassure you that you're on the correct route. It's also beneficial to speak with students who have completed the program before. Ask your university's study abroad office if they can help you connect.

6. **Bonus: Think about enrolling in an online study abroad program:** Last but not least, consider online study abroad programs to broaden your

horizons. Yes, there is such a thing! While an online program may not be the typical way of studying abroad, there are numerous advantages to it that may make it a tempting option for you. Online programs are typically more flexible, accessible, and affordable than their in-person equivalents. Some schools will include hybrid possibilities, so it's worth checking into virtual study abroad programs to see how they can fit into your schedule.

Figure 2.7: Choosing a study abroad program

How to get the information you need

It might be difficult to figure out how to study abroad. For your convenience, I've outlined 10 options (plus a bonus!) that take into consideration various aims and situations to assist you in determining the optimal path.

College and high school students are desiring to study abroad more than ever before, thanks to a plethora of information available on the Internet and social media's love for creating #travelgoals. However, with so many resources come information overload. There isn't just one way to study abroad, which is fortunate for you.

Perhaps your institution is well-known for its excellent exchange program. Perhaps you met someone who had a great time with an immersive experience firm. Maybe someone you follow on Instagram posted an encouraging narrative of their study abroad experience, and you just know you have to go for it.

1. **Enroll in a university-sponsored study abroad program:** Students usually study abroad as part of their college or university education. Study abroad credits are nearly always guaranteed to meet your academic requirements, and primary expenses are generally linked directly to your tuition payments, making them the simplest option to arrange a program. Your university's study abroad program may also handle practicalities such as visas and lodging in addition to offering readily transferrable courses. When it comes to accommodation, did you know that many students claim that studying abroad is less expensive than remaining on campus? By contacting your on-campus program advisor or visiting your school's study abroad web portal, you may learn more about study abroad programs offered via your institution.

2. **Use a third-party service to find study abroad opportunities:** Not all study abroad programs offered by colleges are made equal, just as not all institutions are. If your university doesn't have a program that meets your needs in terms of emphasis, location, or dates, don't quit up and believe you won't be able to study abroad. Regardless of your major or school, there are several firms that operate in the education industry to assist students in spending a semester, year, or summer abroad. Third-party providers are firms that specialize in pairing students with study abroad programs all around the world. One thing to keep in mind is that their services nearly usually come with a program cost. Check with your academic advisor or the study abroad office for suggestions. Universities with few studies abroad choices may have already developed connections with a number of program providers (meaning your credits will transfer smoothly). If your school does not have any existing ties, you can begin your search by going to Go Overseas.

3. **Enroll immediately at an international university:** Another option for studying abroad (that few students consider) is to enroll directly at a university abroad. You can immediately enroll for a semester, year, or complete degree at a university overseas rather than going through an

established program with your home school or a third-party. You may be surprised to learn that you can attend school in another nation even if you are not a citizen of that country. Yes, many overseas students are welcomed with open arms at numerous schools and institutions across the world. That is only one of the many advantages of direct enrollment. If you're applying to a university that doesn't offer English classes, keep in mind that you'll need to have an excellent command of the local language. Not to worry: we've done the legwork for you and compiled a list of English-taught overseas universities. If you want to finish your degree at your home school, be sure the credits from the overseas university are transferable.

4. **Conduct an unbiased worldwide research:** Are you working on a large project or academic paper, and the study abroad programs you've looked into seem too generic? This project might possibly be crucial to the next step of your academic and professional careers. If this describes you, a worldwide independent study abroad might be the answer. Independent studies are generally in-depth courses that a student creates and completes with the help of a faculty sponsor. Brown University, for example, has a fantastic mechanism in place on their website to help students complete the prerequisites for an independent study. While some study abroad programs are comparable to those available via your institution (you'll need to contact a professor, an academic counsellor, and your study abroad office), they differ in size, criteria, and niche emphasis.

5. **Extend your learning by conducting field study in another country:** Do you like active learning situations and can't imagine sitting in yet another classroom (even if it's in another country)? For you, there is a certain sort of study abroad program. Field research is a form of intensive learning experience for potential study abroad students that is ideal for those who find global independent studies to be too difficult. The field experience may not provide as much academic credit as class-based study, but it is still valuable. Consider programs that will allow you to get your hands dirty in archaeological digs or dive off the coast of Malaysia to study marine life. Whatever you're searching for, there's almost certainly a field research program for it.

6. **Work as an intern for academic credit:** You can still intern abroad for school credit before graduation day, even though it is normally regarded the next step after college in order to find a career. Many organizations

throughout the world only hire interns who can earn academic credit, and many colleges need a certain amount of internship credits (also known as hours of experience) in order to graduate. These unpaid pre-entry level positions provide a multitude of learning possibilities while still completing academic requirements. Remember to have your intern program pre-approved to verify that the hours and type of work fit the credit requirements of your home school.

7. **Participate in a student exchange program to study abroad:** Have you ever contemplated trading places with a foreign student for a semester or year to understand what it's like to be in their shoes? You're in luck, since it is a real thing! Student exchanges for study abroad programs are frequently coordinated by "sister schools," or institutions with existing links across the ocean. These colleges will accept a foreign exchange student on the condition that you will be accepted into their school as well. You swap back when both of you have finished your semester or year! Student exchange programs are most frequent at colleges, but they can also be found in high schools. High school exchange programs, which are usually for a shorter period of time, involve language instruction and cultural immersion.

8. **Get a head start by enrolling in a high school study abroad program:** Going abroad in high school is still a popular and practical choice if you want to get a head start on your study abroad adventures and an exchange program isn't an option. High school study abroad programs, which are most popular among graduating seniors, are gaining traction as a viable alternative to college study. You may begin your international education in high school, create connections that will help you in college or in your profession, and obtain a world perspective that will affect the way you regard your own life experiences. Summer and school break programs, as well as the entire year, are available for high school students to study abroad. To get started, look through the hundreds of high school study abroad programs listed on Go Overseas and evaluated by genuine students.

9. **Obtain financial assistance from the federal government in order to study abroad:** Did you know that the Department of State and other government agencies help students of all ages study abroad? You may improve your education and project research by applying to their linked programs whether you're in grades K-12 or at a college or university. Yearlong and summer merit-based scholarships and language programs,

such as the Congress Bundestag Youth Exchange and the National Security Language Initiative for Youth, are available to high school students. Need-based and merit-based scholarships, teaching assistantships, language studies, field research funding, and other opportunities are available to undergraduate and graduate students.

10. **Enroll in a language school in another country:** Enrolling in a language school overseas is another method to study abroad, whether you're still in college, haven't begun, or have already finished. This differs from studying abroad through a third-party provider, as many of them will add extras such as non-language courses, excursions, or connecting you with a local university. Studying abroad with a language school entails taking language lessons, potentially staying with a host family or renting an apartment, and setting off on a new linguistic adventure. Language schools are a popular choice since they are generally less expensive, more enjoyable, and require less paperwork and applications than traditional study abroad programs. Going abroad isn't always possible, whether it's due to a tight academic schedule, a lack of funds, or a global epidemic that has rendered foreign travel impossible (we see you, Coronavirus). However, this does not rule out the possibility of "studying abroad." Virtual study abroad is a new trend that is gaining off at breakneck pace, thanks to a slew of new distance learning technology. Enrolling in a virtual study abroad program allows you to expand your horizons, create international contacts, expand your global network, and immerse yourself in a new culture and language without leaving your home. Sure, you'll miss walking the streets of a new city, but virtual study abroad is a terrific option if conventional study abroad isn't for you. Plus, it's usually a lot less expensive!

11. **Are you prepared to travel abroad?** There is no such thing as the "best" approach to study abroad. Every student's situation is unique, and what works for one may not work for another. Reviewing your selections, evaluating your budget and financial aid opportunities, and selecting the program that best suits your goals is the best method to find the ideal study abroad program for you.

Choosing the country

Studying abroad is a life-changing experience, so take some time to explore before diving into the first place that comes to mind. It's critical to consider all of the advantages and disadvantages of a country where you want to advance your career. We understand how daunting it might be, which is why we've created this book to assist you in choosing your next study destination.

What are your plans for the future?

To begin, list your interests and talents to choose your preferred route of study. Investigate the modules, programs, and durations available for your chosen subject. Also, while you're doing it, look at career opportunities and long-term benefits.

What is the scope of the course you have chosen at your target location?

Understand the industries in which you can find work once you've completed your education. Consider which nations provide the most opportunities for students pursuing your chosen course. Check to see whether the destination has a significant presence in your sector and if any degree of industrial training is offered.

For example, if you want to work in civil engineering, New Zealand is one of the greatest places to go. With the present rise of building projects around the country, civil engineers with attractive benefits are in high demand. Ireland is ideal for healthcare and pharmaceuticals students, whereas Australia is ideal for those looking for research possibilities.

Is the destination's educational system appropriate for you?

Distinct places have different educational structures, which may or may not correspond to your thought process. Examine the instructional methods used in the schools. Many colleges, for example, priorities practical instruction above academic notions. Do you believe this strategy would work for you? Would you be willing to work on research papers and tasks on a weekly basis?

Do you meet the prerequisites for admission?

Always check the admission criteria for the programs offered in your chosen location. Is there a program available at the level you want to start? Is it a certificate or a degree program? Recognize your preferences and make your choices appropriately. Several colleges in Canada, for example, offer a postgraduate certificate rather than a master's degree. In the same way, the United Kingdom provides two types of master's degrees: taught and research.

Check the needed academic scores as well. Do you meet the same criteria? Would you have to take another test in addition to the English proficiency test? Do you believe you'd be able to carve out time in your schedule to study for other exams like the GMAT, GRE, or SAT?

What would it cost you to study at your chosen location?

It is important to assess the whole cost of learning at a given location. Remember to factor in auxiliary expenses like lodging, utilities, and transportation when determining your costs. Consider the length of your course, since this will have a significant impact on the entire cost of studying abroad. For example, master's degrees in the United Kingdom and Ireland are only available for one year, although master's degrees in other countries such as Canada and Australia might last up to two years.

Find out whether there are any government or institute-level scholarships available to study in the targeted location. If you are successful in obtaining one, it will significantly reduce the cost of your courses.

Check to see whether you'll be allowed to work part-time while you're studying so you can keep track of your spending and obtain some professional experience.

Have to decide which course to take?

Did you know that university academic years in other countries differ from those in India? Consider your current situation: can you assemble what you need and apply for the next intake? When applying to a university, gather all of your documentation (such as a Statement of Purpose, Letter of Recommendation, Curriculum Vitae, Transcripts, and so on) and make sure you have everything ready before the start of your selected intake. Consider going for the following intake if you don't have enough time to complete all of these prerequisites.

Are there job opportunities in your destination?

Your selected education should enable you to advance professionally and place you in a position to obtain work. Consider a location that provides a variety of job prospects for your course. For example, if you want to pursue a master's degree in computer science, the United States will provide you with several options. After all, San Diego, San Francisco, Chicago, Boston, and Silicon Valley are all located there.

What are the rules and procedures for student visas?

Check the visa entrance criteria for the place you want to visit. Each nation has its own set of procedures to follow, and visa processing might take longer than anticipated. In addition, visa processing fees differ per nation. Our counsellors can assist you in understanding the visa procedure if necessary.

Is the lifestyle you desire available in your selected location?

Although not a huge element, it is something to consider as an Indian student. The way of life outside of India will be very different. Everything will change, including the language, culture, food, and way of life. Your approach to many circumstances will also shift dramatically.

Consider exploring each destination's way of life to see whether it aligns with your goals.

What is the return on investment and value of your degree in India?

It is normal for an Indian student who would be investing a lot of money, effort, and time to assess the return on investment (ROI). Is the destination going to give you the type of return you're looking for? Is it preparing you for a job? If you're thinking about moving to another nation, think about the prospects and financial benefits. Consider the worth of your degree in your native country, particularly if you want to return. Students considering specialist courses should think about this.

In addition, your University Bureau counsellor will walk you through the logistics of when you may apply to study and when you can start your course in various locations. They may go through your profile in depth and help you map your professional and personal goals to the best nation for you.

Choosing the university

One of the most exciting aspects about selecting to study abroad is that you have a world of options, with hundreds of colleges to choose from all around the world. Each of these colleges will offer dozens, if not hundreds, of different courses, making it difficult to decide what or where you want to study.

Here are seven steps to help you get started on your search for an international university. Before we get into the details, here are some general considerations to keep in mind:

1. **Pay attention to your heart as much as your brain:** They may go in opposite directions, but they both have good points to express. It's often a good idea to start by focusing on what you're enthusiastic about, and then thinking about it thoroughly.
2. **Be truthful to yourself:** Seriously.; any degree is a significant investment, but studying abroad is even more so. Make sure it's something you want to do, not something you feel obligated to do. It will be simpler to persevere through the difficult times if you are doing it because you want to.
3. **Conduct thorough research and consult numerous sources:** A degree can take anything from one to four years to complete, and it can be

rather costly. It will almost probably be a good investment and a life-changing experience, but make sure you are aware of the realities. Official statistics may be found on university websites, and student forums can provide a broader range of viewpoints. If you want to study in the United States, the United Kingdom, or Australia, use the Course Matching Tool, which matches you with the right course and university once you complete a few questions.

4. **Determine your "essential" criteria:** Decide what you really must accomplish or avoid before beginning your quest. Perhaps you only wish to study abroad at an institution where the teaching language is Spanish. Perhaps you have a certain budget or prefer to be only a few hours away from home? It's helpful to establish some specific criteria for your search at this point.

5. **Decide on a subject:** This is where things may become more difficult. Many people know what they want to study right immediately, while for others, the decision is more difficult. If you're unsure what to study, a liberal arts degree, which is known for its more flexible curriculum, is a good option. Great if you already know what you want to study! Some colleges will be ruled out by default (even the most popular topics aren't available everywhere), but you'll be able to choose your favorite institutions based on the courses and curricula they provide. Start by looking at worldwide rankings or university rankings by subject, such as the QS World University Rankings by Subject.

6. **Attend university open days and fairs:** It will take a lot of research to choose the right university overseas for you. Most of this is done online or through university brochures for overseas students. However, the ideal alternative is to visit the campus and/or speak with a university official in person to get a better sense of the school and obtain answers to all of your concerns. While attending open days is frequently challenging for overseas students, it is always worthwhile if you have the opportunity. International university fairs, such as the QS World Grad School Tour, are also excellent places to meet university officials — and instead of attending one open day at a time, you may speak with representatives from numerous schools on the same day. Pre-register for these events to ensure you receive a spot and can fit them into your calendar.

Case study- How to study in Canada

Many students and professionals look to Canada for higher education and work opportunities. People prefer Canada to other countries for their future chances because of its high quality of life and education, which attracts international students seeking opportunities.

Many international students choose to study in Canada because of the country's world-class universities, excellent infrastructure, cultural variety, and career opportunities. Apart from these characteristics, Canada's friendly climate, high-quality lifestyle, and exploration possibilities have made it a popular study destination.

The adaptability, variety, and research of Canada's educational system are well-known. It's worth mentioning that the QS World Rankings for have acknowledged 28 Canadian universities for their brilliance and achievements.

Why Study in Canada?

Canada stands out as a worldwide hub for higher education due to its advanced education sector, rich culture, and beautiful landscapes. Canada is also a peace-loving country where overseas students may feel comfortable and secure.

Canada is one of the most popular study abroad destinations among Indian students. It is also home to a number of well-regarded universities and colleges with reasonable tuition prices. It becomes much more enticing as a result of this. The fact that Canada has some fantastic work prospects is the icing on the cake. In 2021, Canada welcomed a record-breaking 4,50,000 new overseas students. This increase in student enrollment is due to their relaxation of travel limitations and Post-Graduation Work Permit (PWP) criteria. Apart from that, the scenic beauty, racial variety, and warm people make it worthwhile.

Here are some benefits of studying in Canada:

- **Affordable tuition fees and a high level of living**: Canada is affordable in terms of studying and living costs.
- **Home to top universities of the world**: Canada is home to some of the world's best universities, including the University of Toronto, McGill University, University of Waterloo, University of Alberta, and many

others.

- **No language barrier**: English and French are Canada's official languages; surviving there is significantly simpler. English is virtually universally understood, making it perfect for overseas students.
- **High employability rate**: Canada's institutions are well-known for their high graduate employability rates and excellent academic results. The Canadian Ministry of Education encourages overseas students to enroll in Canadian institutions to foster a cosmopolitan atmosphere. This makes it simple for international students to adjust and interact with their peers at college.
- **Internationally recognized educational system**: The university system in Canada is one of the reasons behind the country's excellent academic achievements and inventions. It encourages students to speak up and express themselves without fear of being judged. The lectures are also made engaging to keep the students' attention. Following their examinations, students receive detailed feedback.
- **Immigrant-friendly country**: Canada has welcomed about 15 million immigrants in the last century and a half. In the 1970s, it was also the first country to implement multicultural policies.
- **Financial aid**: The Canadian government provides international students with various financial aid and assistance options. Furthermore, the student visa allows students to work for 20 hours each week while studying in Canada.

How to Study in Canada

If you want to study in Canada and eventually become a permanent resident, follow the steps below.

- **Choose a program:** Conduct research to identify the education program in Canada that you wish to pursue.
- **Apply to a Canadian designated learning institution:** Once you've decided the education program you want to apply to, send your application to the designated learning institution (DLI) of your choice in Canada.
- **Apply for a study permit:** After receiving a letter of acceptance, Cohen Immigration Law may assist you in submitting an application for a study

permit to the Government of Canada. The study permit is a document that most individuals require in order to stay in Canada lawfully as a student.

- **Investigate your immigration options:** After you've finished your courses, Cohen Immigration Law can assist you in staying in Canada to get further professional job experience and apply for permanent residency.

What are the Benefits of Studying in Canada?

With over 600,000 foreign students, Canada has become one of the world's most popular locations for international students. International students are drawn to Canada for the following reasons, according to research:

- High-quality education provided by Canadian schools
- Opportunities for international students to work during and after their studies, as well as transition to permanent residence
- Studying in English and/or French
- Safety and security
- Multicultural society
- Canada welcomes immigrants and international students from nearly 200 countries each year
- Canada is affordable when compared to other popular international student destinations.

Study in Canada requirements

You should be aware of the prerequisites for studying in Canada if you consider traveling there for higher education. Even if different schools and courses have varied criteria and expectations, most universities that provide academic master's degrees for overseas students have certain common requirements.

- The preferred university's application form, filled out completely.
- Official transcripts and documents proving a prior degree;

- Official documentation confirming professional designations, if relevant;
- Two (2) letters of academic recommendation attesting to graduate school preparation;
- A complete chronological résumé clearly describing educational achievements, job experience and growth, and other similar experiences;
- Letters from employers attesting to a degree of experience and analytical writing abilities for individuals without recent academic experience;
- A Letter of Intent (LOI) that explains why the student is applying and specifies his or her academic goals.
- If the candidate provides a certification from an unrecognized school, a credential examination from a recognized agency proving equivalence is needed by the Admissions Committee;
- Proof of proficiency in the English language.
- Scores on the GMAT or GRE for MBA and Master's programs in Canada.
- You must submit TCF, TEF, DELF, and DALF French Proficiency Tests if you are applying to a French-taught program.
- Evidence that you have the money to study in Canada.
- English Proficiency Tests Accepted: IELTS, PTE, TOEFL

Best alternatives to IELTS for studying in Canada:

- Include scores from supplementary English proficiency assessments, such as the TOEFL and PTE.
- You can study in Canada without taking the IELTS if you have spent at least four years in an English-medium school and can demonstrate this through your academic qualifications.
- Enroll in the university's English language program.
- Citizens of English-speaking nations are excused from giving IELTS scores in Canada.

Top Universities to Study in Canada without IELTS

Alternatives to English assessments such as TOEFL, Duolingo English Test, and PTE are readily available to students wishing to study in Canada. Some

Canadian institutions enable students to show documentation of their English proficiency, such as a school English certificate, or to enroll in an English language course. IELTS scores are not required for students from English-speaking countries. Here is a list of popular universities in Canada where you may study without taking the IELTS exam.

- University of Winnipeg
- Brock University
- University of Saskatchewan
- Memorial University of Newfoundland and Labrador
- Cambrian University
- Okanagan College
- Concordia University
- Seneca College
- Carleton University

Popular Intakes

Universities in Canada provide three major entrance points or intakes for applicants to study. Fall, Winter, and Summer are the three seasons. Fall is the most popular intake season in the country, followed by Winter and Summer. Because of the limited courses and people applying to colleges, the summer intake is the least popular.

Education System

Canada's education system includes public and private institutions that provide high-quality education. Over 10,000 graduate and undergraduate programs in Canada are offered by 213 public colleges and 223 public and private universities. Universities in Canada offer the following degrees:

- **Undergraduate Degree:** In Canada, a bachelor's degree is pursued following the 12th-grade competition. The course type and province determine the length of the program. In Canada, however, most undergraduate degrees are four years long.
- **Associate Degree:** An associate degree is an undergraduate degree that entails one or two years of study in a particular topic or profession. These

programs, however, differ significantly from one institution to the next and from one region to the next.

- **Graduate Degree:** A graduate degree is a Master of Arts or Master of Science. A master's degree takes between two and three years to complete in Canada.
- **Ph.D.:** In Canada, a doctorate, sometimes known as a Ph.D., is a specialized post-graduate degree that can take anywhere from three to six years to complete.

Credit System in Canada

In Canada, all universities follow the same credit system. To compute the outcome, the credits earned by a student during the course are taken into account.

- An undergraduate degree/degree Bachelor's takes 3-5 credits for each course. A Bachelor's degree typically requires 90-120 credit hours to complete.
- Three to four credits for each course for a Master's degree. In Canada, a Master's degree requires around 30 credits or more.
- The grade point average, or GPA, is a measure that ranges from 0.0 to 4.0 that is used in the Canadian educational system to grade students. These are generated for each semester based on the grades received in each course and the credits acquired for that semester. A grade of 4.0 corresponds to an A, whereas a grade of 0.0 corresponds to an F.

Cost of studying and living in Canada

Though it isn't on the list of requirements, the cost of studying and living in Canada is a key issue for many people before they consider studying abroad. Housing, food, health insurance, travel, and tuition fees are all included in Canada's total cost of education.

- **Tuition fees:** Tuition costs are influenced by the type of qualification and the university of choice. Every year, the cost of studying in Canada is estimated to be between CAD 7,000 and CAD 35,000. The cost varies depending on the type of course you take.

- **Accommodation:** Colleges provide on-campus housing for international students. Students who choose to live off-campus can do so in shared apartments with other students. On-campus housing can cost anywhere from CAD 8,000 to CAD 10,000 per year, whereas a shared apartment might cost anywhere from CAD 400 to CAD 700 per month, depending on where you live and when you go. It might cost up to CAD 1000 to CAD 2000 each month in the most attractive areas and cities.
- **Living costs:** In Canada, a single student budget might range from CAD 6,000 to CAD 10,000, based on various expenses and living costs, including communication, transportation, books and supplies, daily essentials, and so on.
- **Miscellaneous:** The visa and study permits will set you back around CAD 150. The cost of health and insurance varies from CAD 300 to CAD 800 per year. The above cost ranges are the fundamental cost ranges to give you a sense of what it costs to plan appropriately.

Scholarships to Study in Canada

Merit-based scholarships are also available at Canadian universities for students who are unable to pay for their education. When applying for scholarships, keep the following in mind:

- The majority of awards need a good academic score. This, however, varies by city, subject, and grade level.
- Each college receives a different amount of money. Because scholarship applications take time, you should start the procedure at least 8 to 12 months before the start of the course.

Here is a list of scholarships available to students studying in Canada:

1. Vanier Canada Graduate Scholarships
2. Ontario Trillium Scholarship
3. Ontario Graduate Scholarship
4. Go Clean Scholarship
5. Humber College International Entrance Scholarship
6. Waterloo Merit Scholarship

7. UBC International Leader of Tomorrow Award
8. Science and Law School Scholarship
9. Quebec Provincial Government Scholarship
10. University of Manitoba Graduate Fellowships

If you don't have enough funds to study in Canada, you may always take out an education loan. It takes a lot of time and work to get a loan approved. As soon as you obtain confirmation from the university, you must apply for a loan as quickly as possible. You should compute the amount you will be requesting for the loan after you have an estimate of your expenses, including studies and living. Before applying for a loan, do some research to see which banks are offering the greatest prices.

Affordable Universities in Canada

International students can enroll in a variety of affordable university programs in Canada. The best university in Canada with the lowest tuition prices are listed below.

- Brandon University
- University of Guelph
- Memorial University of Newfoundland
- Canadian Mennonite University
- University of St. Boniface
- McGill University
- Humber College
- University of Calgary
- University of Northern British Columbia
- Centennial College

Course options in Canada

In Canada, there are several course alternatives to choose from. Universities provide a high-quality education with internationally recognized degrees. Bachelor's, Master's, Doctoral, Diploma, and Certificate degrees are available in Canada. International students can choose their preferred program level. The top Canadian universities provide a variety of programs at each level.

Canada's top programs include business and finance, nursing, dentistry, engineering, and pharmacy. Management, engineering, health, science, media, journalism, and many more areas have courses available at various levels. In Canada, courses range from entry-level to top-of-the-line programs that combine straightforward approaches with on-field applications. In Canada, courses incorporate the most up-to-date educational methodologies, including the latest in technical advancement and practical application.

- **Business and Finance:** When it comes to international applicants, business management degrees are the most popular. The MBA program is one of the most popular in this industry. Banking, management consulting, and investment finance are all industries that never go out of vogue. The need for management heads in many economic areas continues to rise. However, it is preferable to specialize in Statistics, Accounting, or Finance than to get a standard MBA because it has more specialized value. McGill University, Centennial College, Humber College, and Concordia University are the finest places to look.
- **Nursing:** Nursing is the second most popular healthcare career among overseas students. Although a certificate or an undergraduate degree in nursing are both available, it is usually preferable to pursue the latter. Emergency nursing, pediatric nursing, oncology nursing, and other specialist nursing courses are available. Registered nurses must have completed a school nursing program and passed a national licensure test. It should be mentioned that to be eligible for a Master's degree in Nursing in Canada, you must have 1-2 years of practical experience as a registered nurse. Toronto University, Alberta University, McMaster University, and others are among the finest nursing schools in the area.
- **Dentistry:** Dentistry is one of the most well-paid professions in Canada. To begin practicing, however, one must have exceptionally high credentials and, as a result, several years of school in the same subject. Instead of becoming a general practitioner, it is also feasible to specialize in fields such as Oral Pathology, Orthodontics, or Pediatric Dentistry after completing a master's degree. In order to qualify for a DDS (Doctor of Dental Surgery) or a DMD, one must pass the DAT, or Dental Aptitude Test, in addition to the associated undergraduate course (Doctor of Medicine in Dentistry).

- **Engineering:** Engineering and the information technology industry have traditionally been highly recognized in Canada. Software or Computer Engineering, Mechanical Engineering, and Chemical Engineering are some of the greatest courses. This industry pays the greatest wages in and around Central Canada, particularly in Ontario and Quebec. Those with industry-standard software skills are assured employment with salaries that never fall below $51,000, with the majority of employees earning more than that. Toronto University, the University of Waterloo, McGill University, and McMaster University are the top engineering schools in Canada.
- **Pharmacy:** This profession necessitates a high level of expertise. Most persons working in this profession in Canada have at least a PhD degree. It is mostly a research-based field. There are also a range of employment alternatives available, such as community pharmacist, hospital pharmacist, educational institution pharmacist, and so on. To become a pharmacist, you must have a lot of practical experience. International Pharmacy Graduates, or IPGs, must follow their own set of rules in order to obtain licensure in Canada. Toronto University, the University of British Columbia, and the Bredin Institute are all relevant institutions.

How to apply for a study visa in Canada?

International students can study in Canada at recognized learning institutes with a Study Permit. Before applying for the permission, make sure you have all the necessary documentation. A study permit isn't the same as a visa. A temporary resident visa must be applied for individually. A study permit is valid for the term of your course plus an additional 90 days. This extra time allows you to depart or request an extension.

Before you arrive to Canada, you need to apply for a study permit. Only a few persons are eligible to apply for a study permit in Canada. Additionally, you can apply when you arrive in Canada.

Applying online is one alternative for submitting an application. The permission is completed quickly with the online application, preventing any delays. If they require any more papers, they may be added online instantly, saving time from having to courier them. You may also use your account to stay up to date on the status of your application.

When applying for a study visa, you must submit the following documents:

- Proof of university acceptance
- Proof of identity, including a valid passport, pictures, and any other identifying documents
- Proof of financial assistance, such as proof of college loan or a bank statement from the last four months, or any other document that meets the criteria.

Essential documents for Canadian Student Visa:

Once you get a letter of admission from the college, you should apply for a student visa. You should start the visa application procedure as soon as possible. The following documents are required for this:

1. **Valid passport:** To apply for a Study Permit, you must have a valid passport. According to the Canadian High Commission, you must have a passport that is valid for the period of your anticipated stay in Canada, which is at least your course term.
2. **Proof of the institute's acceptance:** You'll need the admission letter from the university or institute. A Designated Learning Institute is one that has been approved by the Immigration Department.
3. **Proof of funds:** You'd have to produce proof of your financial situation. Its purpose is to demonstrate that you are financially capable of covering both your tuition and living expenses. A student must produce a minimum of $10,000 in Canadian funds for each year of their stay in Canada, according to Canadian Immigration.
4. **Photographs in passport size:** According to the guidelines, you'll require two passport-sized pictures.
5. **Immigration medical exam (IME):** International students from India are required by Canadian Immigration to complete a mandatory Immigration Medical Examination by impaneled doctors. It is recommended that they schedule an appointment with one of the specified physicians for a medical checkup at least a week before they begin their Visa application. This allows the doctor sufficient time to review and upload the necessary documentation.

6. **Score on the english language proficiency exam:** For admission to a Canadian university, you must submit your English language proficiency score. TOEFL, IELTS, are all recognized.

7. **Statement of purpose:** When applying for a Canadian Study Permit, you must submit a statement explaining the objective of your trip and why you chose this specific institute.

8. **Credit card:** The fee for applying for a visa in Canada is CAD $160, and it must be paid online. The system will only take credit cards. If you're filling out an online application, you'll need to scan all of the above-mentioned documents and upload them digitally. If you want to fill out an application offline, you'll need genuine copies of all of the above documents. A large number of Canadian colleges are known for having a global viewpoint, since they provide opportunity for students from all backgrounds and nations to interact with one another, learn from one another, and share ideas, resulting in a cosmopolitan culture in the institution. After Graduating from any of the programs of studies, you may be able to work temporarily in Canada to gain some work experience. For this, you will have to apply for a work permit which later on qualifies you for a permanent residence. There are certain norms that have to be followed for this procedure. And, although these are long term plans but if you apply for a Post-Graduation Work Permit, you may be allowed to work in Canada for up to three years after you graduate. After graduating from one of the programs, you may be eligible to work in Canada for a period of time to gain experience. To do so, you'll need to apply for a work permit, which will eventually qualify you for permanent residency. For this, there are few guidelines that must be followed. Although these are long-term ambitions, you may be able to work in Canada for up to three years after graduation if you apply for a Post-Graduation Work Permit.

Study Pathways to Permanent Residence (PR)

International students who complete post-secondary education in Canada have several options for extending their stay and eventually moving to Canada permanently.

When it comes to securing permanent residency in Canada, your education in Canada may provide you an edge. Candidates with Canadian education and job experience are valued in several federal and provincial immigration schemes.

You can earn Canadian work experience after completing your studies in Canada by acquiring a Post-Graduation Work Permit (PGWP), which allows you to work in Canada for up to three years depending on your Canadian academic degree.

You can then seek a number of federal and provincial permanent residency options while holding a PGWP, including:

Express Entry

Submitting an Express Entry profile is one of the most popular ways to apply for permanent residence. Express Entry is Canada's primary system for processing economic immigration applications.

The Comprehensive Ranking System is used to evaluate Express Entry applicants. Candidates that are young, have Canadian education and job experience, and have high English and/or French fluency are rewarded by the Comprehensive Ranking System. Many international students in Canada exhibit these qualities.

Former international students may be eligible for the famous Canadian Experience Class (CEC) program, which allows tens of thousands of former international students and temporary foreign employees to become permanent citizens each year, thanks to Express Entry.

Provincial Nominee Program (PNP)

The Provincial Nominee Program (PNP) permits provinces and territories across Canada to find immigrants who match their specific economic requirements. Many PNP streams honors candidates who have worked with foreign students in the past or who are committed to help international students.

Quebec

Quebec is Canada's second-largest province, and Montreal, its capital, is a favorite foreign student destination. The province has its own immigration system, with programs that differ from those given by the federal government and those covered by the PNP. Former international students are also encouraged to make the move to permanent residency in Quebec. The Quebec Experience Program is one of the main ways it aims to do this.

Other Federal Programs

The federal government controls other economic class immigration programs in addition to the three Express Entry categories. International students can take advantage of specific tracks in the programs, as well as waivers from Canadian work experience requirements. The Atlantic Immigration Program and the Rural and Northern Immigration Pilot are two of them.

III

Preparations to study abroad

Making the decision to study abroad is a crucial one for academic success. As a result, you must make a number of important decisions with the assistance of your family and professional mentors before you start working toward your desire. You may start by doing a lot of research and talking to people about your study-abroad ambitions.

Here are a few things to consider straight away:

- Choosing the right nation, college, or university
- Selecting the appropriate semester
- Selecting a school
- Getting letters of acceptance
- Accommodation
- Visa

Given all of these considerations, it is prudent to plan ahead of time for your studies abroad. To ensure a smooth procedure, begin working and systematically executing this strategy 1 to 1.5 years in advance.

Academic objectives

There is a reason why "study abroad" isn't the same as "give up all things learning and just get credit for nothing." You should research and even create goals for your study abroad experience. To maintain focus and make the most of your time studying abroad, set a reasonable number of personal academic goals.

Figure 3.1: Academic objectives to study abroad

What academic objectives do you want to achieve by studying abroad?

The following academic goals for studying abroad:

- **Avoid procrastinating.** Finish your homework on time (or, dare we say, ahead of schedule).
- **Go to lectures.** Wait until you have access to Wednesday departures on absurdly cheap plane tickets to London before you realize how challenging college is?
- **Finishall of your homework**, including the reading. Give yourself plenty of time to review and ponder your work.

Figure 3.2: Academic goals for studying abroad

- **Set a grade-related goal for yourself.** A 4.0 GPA could be a noteworthy souvenir from your semester abroad.
- **Record your notes.** Although active note-taking and active listening are both advantageous, the latter is significantly more so.
- **Create a space just for studying.** This could be a nearby café, a calm area of the library at your distant university, or even your dorm room.
- **Get enough sleep and take care of yourself.** When studying abroad, there is nothing wrong with integrating self-care into your academic objectives. Feeling your best can help you focus, remember material, and perform well on exams.
- **Think about taking an internship.** The opportunity for real-world application provided by overseas practical experience makes for a

formidable combination with theoretical understanding.

- **Enroll in a language course.** Immersion is paramount!
- **Enroll in a language class covering a different subject.** Do you actually want to get better at Spanish? This is a significant advancement.
- Schedule at least one meeting with each instructor during the course of your program. Being more than just another student in their class has a number of benefits.
- Read a few novels set in the country where you are studying abroad. These can be on any subject as long as they add to the background information for your new home.
- **Participate in class.** Raise your hand, take part in discussions, and answer that question you're an asked...
- Write more than the basic minimum for one paper. You obtain a 100 on every test you take. Encourage yourself to go beyond what is "good enough."
- **Time management.** While studying abroad, schedule time in your daily schedule to complete all of your academic objectives!

Making connections

Whether you are an online or on-campus international student, networking will be an essential component of your academic experience. You can meet people in your field through networking who share your interests, skills, connections, and experiences. It will help you while looking for work if you can build a solid professional network early in your career.

There is no need to worry, even though face-to-face networking can seem to be limited in the current context. Through the internet, you may still put your skills to use and interact with others around the globe.

Figure 3.3: Making connections to study abroad

How to properly network while studying online It's acceptable if you're scared to network with your lecturers and students due to the widespread use of online learning. Follow these straightforward networking advices to pave the way for a prosperous career:

- **Sign up for events online:** Enroll in seminars, town hall meetings, and online courses to make it simpler to meet new people. Look for research volunteer roles at your university or in your town to gain work experience and meet new people.
- **Establish a professional network online:** To start building your network, introduce yourself to your professors and students via email

or social media. Zoom, Google Meet, or Skype are examples of free video conferencing tools that may be used to facilitate meetings and real-time conversations. You can communicate with alumni from your university on social media and learn from their experiences by doing so. Additionally, they could be able to help you launch your career.

- **Create a presence online:** To build your online visibility, create a profile on a business networking site like LinkedIn. Your professional profile will grow as a result, and you'll have a great chance to network with potential employers. Making an online portfolio that shows your abilities, expertise, and skills is a great idea. You can post this on your online networking networks to showcase your effort.

- **Take part in pertinent online forums:** Many paid and free online communities, including Reddit forums and GitHub, can help you interact with like-minded people and keep up with industry news. Use these to draw connections within your area of interest.

- **Participate in online discussion boards for the classroom:** Most institutions that provide online classes also maintain chat rooms or online communities for particular assignments or projects. Utilize this chance to interact with your classmates. Talk about your ideas and strike up a dialogue. You can use this to help you establish your unique voice and personality among your peers. Remember to plan your presentation of your thoughts if an assignment calls for a group discussion. Not outsmarting others should be the aim, but rather standing out. These recommendations may seem simple, but we assure you that if you adhere to them strictly, you will have a substantial professional network by the time you graduate.

Managing your expectations

- **In advance of studying abroad:** Your parents may provide the biggest obstacle for you once you realise you have this once-in-a-lifetime opportunity to study abroad. Both before and after you go, your family will be looking out for you. They are simply keeping an eye on you because they want everything to go smoothly; they are not intentionally trying to irritate or annoy you. Because you'll be far away from them, they might be curious about what you'll be doing, where you'll be, and who you'll be with all the time. Set up a plan of communication before you leave to ensure them that you will stay in touch. Check in when you get there, whenever you have internet access, or within the first 24 hours.

- **Expectations for your study abroad experience:** Now that you are halfway around the world away from any familiar faces, you could feel lonely. You are not alone, in fact, the opposite is true, so relax. With students from your home country and other international students from all around the world, you will study abroad. There are new opportunities to meet new folks every day. If you have any concerns, problems, or just need someone to talk to, you can always rely on the staff, representatives, and locals who are present to support you and provide you with advice. These brand- new relationships and memories will endure forever!

Following a study abroad experience, one should anticipate:

You might experience both small and significant life changes when you get back home, but here's the catch: they will all be for the better! You'll see that you're energised and enthusiastic about life. You recently returned from studying abroad in a country that is entirely different from your own; the events you saw and the experiences you had sparked your curiosity about the rest of the world.

You will notice and welcome change, which will give you a completely new perspective on the world. You will realise that studying abroad for even a short time—say, a few months—can truly encourage your personal growth on all levels—spiritual, intellectual, and emotional. People will notice your increasing maturity, and the "new you" might encourage others to eventually study abroad.

Health and safety

Your success and health when travelling overseas are important to the University Bureau's Health and Safety Team. Planning is necessary if you require medication or have a pre-existing condition because access and resources will differ abroad.

My team will guide you through the pre-departure process and put you in touch with the best foreign medical facilities.

Before selecting a program, evaluate your general health to ascertain your physical, mental, and emotional needs.

- Make a health plan for your time spent travelling. How will you stay in good mental, emotional, and physical health while completing your program? What habits, supports, or coping techniques will you use to do this?
- Get the CDC- and/or a doctor's recommended vaccines and preventive medications before flying to your destination. Prior to your arrival, several governments demand or advise vaccines or other particular treatments. Look into this as soon as you can because these may need to be done in a series spanning several months. The International Society of Travel Medicine (ISTM) has a database of qualified travel medicine professionals.

Communicating with your family

Are you thinking about going overseas to school but are concerned that it would be difficult to stay in touch with your loved ones back home? With some preparation and the aid of technology, maintaining relationships back home is now simpler than ever. Following are four tried-and-true suggestions from rajan arya (rajanarya.com) on how to stay in touch with loved ones while studying abroad.

1. **Sharing your life via social media with your family and friends while studying abroad**: You'll meet new people and make friends while studying abroad, so it's easy to have a full academic and social schedule, but remember to regularly schedule regular time for chats and video calls with your family and loved ones back home. After all, you want to stay in touch with your family and friends while studying abroad, as well as your new friends studying abroad. Your family can still keep up with your daily life via video chats or group chats on WhatsApp or iMessage while you're abroad. Letting your family and friends follow you on social media platforms like Instagram as well is also a nice way of keeping in touch with everyone back home when you're away. Your parents and friends will also be concerned about your safety while studying abroad. This will be a great way to have local popular chat apps downloaded and add your family there in cases where the overseas connections are unstable. Additionally, you could use tools such as WhatsApp to connect your family members with your closest friends in the host country, so

they can still reach you in case of an emergency.

2. **Calculating and keeping in mind the time zone difference when studying abroad**: Staying in touch with family and friends while you're studying abroad in a different time zone presents a few extra challenges. You'll either wake up to messages from well-meaning family members or risk disturbing their sleep. One strategy to internalize the time difference is to keep one of your electronic devices, such as a laptop or tablet, on your home city's time zone until you adjust. If you find that too confusing, try getting in the habit of checking world time zones on your mobile's clock. This will be useful in the future as you stay in touch with your other friends studying abroad from around the world. Usually, weekends are the most convenient time for people in different time zones.

3. **Drop them postcards from your location**: We know, snail mail seems so last century. But, don't you get a little excited when you get a hand-written note from someone you miss? It feels extra-special and postcards are an opportunity to share a little memento of your experiences. Sharing experiences and lit-up moments with those back home will help you stay in touch with family and friends while you're studying abroad. Postcards from national parks, museums, and old towns and cities with a few lines from you about a funny experience or little discovery will make your loved ones feel like they're exploring with you. The postcards you send from your host country with details of your study abroad experiences to your family can be a great, warm way of keeping in touch with your family, letting them know how much you love and miss them when you study abroad.

4. **Keep a study abroad blog to share your experience with people from home**: You will always gain some valuable experiences from studying abroad. Your family and friends back home will be your travel blog's most dedicated readers as they watch you explore a new country, make lifelong friends, and maybe live a bit vicariously through all of the delicious foods and exotic scenery. Many students start travel blogs while they study abroad but few keep them through the entirety of their studies as they quickly become too busy to update their blogs. Getting grandma to sign up for Facebook, and dad to make an Instagram account can be a great way of making sure everyone's included even when you're short on time.

5. **Don't forget to schedule plans back home while studying abroad**: It's easy (and healthy) to have such a great time studying abroad that you forget to make plans with your loved ones back home. If you're studying abroad for an extended period, you can make plans to visit home, invite your friends and family to your new country for a visit, or discover a new country together. While studying, it's normal to miss people back home, and having a plan in place is an excellent way to keep in touch with family and friends and stop feeling homesick abroad. As you near the end of a semester, year, or longer, remember to plan homecoming celebrations with your nearest and dearest to catch up.

Get the most out of your experience

Studying abroad may be difficult, enjoyable, terrifying, and fantastic all at the same time. Make sure to utilise your international studies to the fullest. Here are our top suggestions.

- **Never does the dream equal reality:** When you study abroad, one thing is certain: Your experience won't be what you expected it to be. It will be unique. Even when you study abroad, there are certain mundane ordinary days, and at first, you could feel a little lonely. However, you will meet a lot of new individuals once your lessons begin. Most students find that the longer they study abroad, the more they like it.
- **Keep calm and don't panic:** It's common to worry what you've gotten yourself into on the first night of studying abroad, as I have done myself countless times. Just hours after arriving, I've witnessed students lose control and leave the school without giving it a fair chance or even setting foot inside.
- **Check to be sure it's not you!** Be prepared for the reality that your living situation, your school, and the city may not quite match your expectations, and that it could take some time to make friends. Arriving the week before classes begin is typically plenty, especially if you're travelling alone. In this way, you won't have to spend as much time alone before classes begin and will have access to a social setting where you may meet new people.
- **Stay active to stave against homesickness:** Spend as little time as possible conversing with friends and relatives when alone in your room.

That's a simple way to start missing home. Go outside and discover your new nation and city. Be engaged by enrolling in school- sponsored events and participating in ones that your friends are planning. Say "yes"! Even though you will ultimately go back home, you can only fully appreciate your study abroad experience right now!

- **Maximize your academic efforts:** Of course, studying is a major component of studying abroad. So keep it in mind and make every effort to learn. You want to be fluent in French when you return home after completing a language course in France, don't you? Then you must work hard and also study in your spare time. Make sure to take your studies seriously; you will feel much better and yet have time for enjoyment.

- **Set objectives and create a strategy to meet them** What motivates your desire to study abroad? What do you want to accomplish and encounter? Before you go and before you make a school decision, give your ambitions some thought. Your options and experience will be very different from those of someone who just wants to have fun and see the globe if your objective is to enhance your CV and spend a year studying at the best institution available. There are no right or wrong answers, but it's still a good idea to consider what you want to see and do before travelling, even if it's just for the experience. When you are away from home, keep your goals in mind and consider how you will accomplish them. Without a plan, there is a chance that time will pass and it will soon be time to return home. By the time it happens, it will be too late to do everything you had planned, so get to work today.

- **Network and develop lifelong friends:** When studying abroad, the majority of people seek out new acquaintances. Try to build relationships with individuals; it will be beneficial and help you better comprehend various cultures. You could meet your future spouse, make lifelong friends, or locate a business partner. If you get to know a professor, they could be willing to serve as your reference in the future if you apply for employment or to other colleges. Don't forget to update your CV to reflect your international studies and any employment you may have held there.

- **A wonderful time:** Studying abroad is a fantastic way to travel and develop personally. Make the most of your time abroad and remember to have fun since you will likely look back on this time with fondness in the future!

Understanding the culture

You will spend a lot of time being urged to get ready for your study abroad adventure and adjusting to a new culture. It's crucial to understand that almost everyone goes through a time of transition. Coming home may occasionally be just as frightening as being abroad.

It certainly feels similar to when you first arrived in your host nation when you return home. You can realize that you have changed and that home no longer seems natural and comfortable.

Following your study abroad experience, you could have the following emotions:

- Joy at being at home with loved ones and friends
- Boredom
- Trouble communicating how you feel about your experiences
- Relationship understanding has changed, and you're having trouble comprehending your culture (norms, values, negative views, etc.)
- Difficulty in putting information or new skills to use (foreign language, etc.)
- Must understand new cultural nuances (slang, cultural references, etc.)

There is no set method to acclimate; your experience is your own. Even while there are some typical feelings you could experience after travelling overseas, everyone's response to returning home is unique. Recognize that these emotions are common and a constant aspect of your cross-cultural experience.

While you were away, you changed, and now you're in a situation where those changes are obvious. Cultural readjustment is navigating this new you with others who remember the old you, not going back to the way you were before your study abroad experience.

Strategies for managing re-entry

Here are some exclusive tips from former study abroad students: Recovery requires time. Think about the three Ps: Be Patient, Present, and Proactive, if you're in a rut.

- **Be persistent:** It may take days, weeks, or even longer to readjust. A virtue for studying abroad is patience. Not everyone will share your experiences and understanding. You might need to do some "cultural catching up," such as picking up new terminology or keeping up with current affairs and pop culture.
- **Be there:** Beginning your daily routine back home may seem dull in comparison to living abroad, but remember that ordinary events may still be exciting! Share your experiences, but don't let them consume you. You have an entire life to live and if you want, you can continue it abroad. Stay in the here and now. Negative feeling about your home culture can be expected. Making comparisons between cultures and nations is natural; however, be careful of being too critical in comparisons or generalizations.
- **Be Proactive:** Make a strategy and take risks. Decide what you must do for yourself, and then take action. If you require Join a club, organize a language exchange group, and get to know the visiting foreign students. Once you've returned to UW-Madison, speak with your academic or study abroad adviser.

If you're having a hard time adjusting, seek help.

Speak to someone if you ever feel like you might use some assistance managing reentry effects (such as more strong emotions for a longer amount of time).

Signs that you should think about consulting a professional include:

- Depression or ongoing melancholy
- Dramatic changes in eating or sleeping habits
- Low energy or physical tiredness; lack of desire or interests; anxiety and excessive worrying; loneliness, helplessness, or hopelessness; thoughts of oneself or other harmful activity; behavioral changes
- Reentry's ups and downs are to be expected and often pass with time. Taking the time to analyses what your study abroad experience means for your future is a part of your readjustment.

Getting involved

It might be difficult to explain your study abroad experience to loved ones, close friends, and potential employers. On the other hand, if you haven't given it any consideration, you can't talk about it. It's crucial to give your communication of your study abroad experience some thought. By doing this, you may increase the effect and draw on the connections you've built between other nations, cultures, and cross- cultural abilities. The basis for telling your story will be laid by understanding what made your experience special.

Apply your newly acquired talents as you advance academically, professionally, and personally after your study abroad experience.

Personal and cultural identity

Students studying abroad must adapt to a new cultural environment that includes various historical and cultural understandings of inclusion and diversity with regard to matters like race and ethnicity, gender identity, religion, and disability. There are probably different social norms, laws, amenities, and customs abroad. Students frequently worry about how they will be viewed in the nation they are studying in. Students occasionally experience what it's like to be the minority for the first time. Some people worry that their experience will be impacted by their color, language, ethnicity, religion, gender, etc.

Consider what it will be like to be "you" there. In the nation you are visiting, these definitions could be altered, and you might run across prejudices, inquiries, and enquirers over your identities. Be ready if your experiences cause you to feel frustrated, lonely, or worn out by weighing your expectations against what could really happen overseas. Despite the difficulties, keep in mind that adjusting to a new culture is a great chance for development and transformation. It will also provide you a fresh perspective on how other cultures are organized.

A few things you can do to get ready are listed below:

- Research the history, culture, legal system, and population of the host nation. Consider the perspective of the author while reading news items, commentary, or blogs. Speak to students who have studied abroad in your host country.

- Make advantage of internet resources that provide guidance, personal accounts, and other information (including social media, which may be less "screened" than news sources in certain countries or may highlight current events/stories that aren't "news-worthy").

Cross cultural communication

Many of us find it difficult to deal with persons whose English is weak, whether intentionally or unconsciously. Whether we like to acknowledge it or not, some of us feel that talking to them is a waste of our time. It takes intentionality to interact with them. We are more prone to miss individuals whose English is weak if we are not thinking about it. We need to intentionally listen to them and be conscious of our own biases. We must urge others to engage if we genuinely appreciate their viewpoints.

It's crucial for an international student to remain objective and polite while meeting people from different backgrounds.

You'll meet a variety of students from all backgrounds during your study abroad journey. Your ability to remain grounded throughout your studies will increase with a greater sense of cultural awareness.

International students frequently face culture shock when they first enrol in a foreign institution. It might be difficult to acclimatise at first since your surroundings are so different from those you are used to.

Although many students perceive culture shock as a bad thing, it can also turn out to be beneficial. You may extend your thinking and get new perspectives by exposing your heart and head to another culture.

Why does that benefit you?

In a professional sense, it demonstrates to potential employers that you are a self-assured person who isn't frightened of taking on new challenges, even if they are located on the other side of the globe!

It also reveals how patient you are. You maintain your resiliency in the face of uncertainty and doubt, enhancing your character and promoting the development of your growth attitude.

Why is intercultural communication seen as an important study skill?

Many international students have gone through their study abroad experience without instruction on the cultural norms and values of the host nation.

As an alternative, there are people who encountered cultural bias, ignorance, and bigotry while attending university and had no one to talk to or confront them about it.

This can be due to the dearth of study skills classes that emphasise the value of intercultural communication.

You'll be able to express yourself with confidence and learn how to be patient with others who don't share your background if you develop cross-cultural communication skills.

Additionally, it will provide you a wonderful chance to interact with students from various countries and talk about your differences. Exciting community activities and gatherings may be held as a result of bringing up the subject of cross-cultural dialogue, which is also an excellent opportunity to sample delectable foods and drinks from various countries!

In the end, intercultural communication promotes fair judgement and equitable chances. Students who don't include it in their university study skills classes are missing out on useful methods and strategies for the future.

Research culture and law

The Faculty of Legal is always seeking to establish and uphold collaborative relationships with the top law faculties and institutions throughout the globe.

International research and educational partnership is a priority for the faculty of law. We have collaborated with some of the top legal colleges and institutions around the world to make studying abroad possible for our students as well as to attract students from all over the world to our faculty and establish an international campus. In addition to the numerous institutional collaborations with the University of Bergen, students and researchers gain from the more than 150 foreign academic partners.

We are adamant that spending a semester or a whole year abroad broadens students' perspectives, imparts important knowledge about other legal systems and cultures, and offers them access to an international network that will be helpful to them in their future professional lives. Additionally, while they study foreign laws and legal systems, the students simultaneously develop their knowledge of and sensitivity to the distinctive features of Norwegian law and legal culture.

In the past several years, between 40 and 50 percent of students earning a Master of Law from the University of Bergen have studied abroad for a semester or an entire year.

Case Study UK Education System

Engineering, science, art and design, business and management, law, and finance are just a few subjects where the UK is a global leader in education. Some of the brightest minds in the world are drawn to the UK because of its reputation and history as a global hub for scientific research. The UK produces 8% of all scientific papers worldwide, with just 1% of the global population.

The UK provides a famous educational system with degrees that may change your destiny. Every year, it draws more than 600,000 international students to various programs, from PhDs to English language classes.

The UK educational system allows students to mix and match classes and subjects from many academic fields, allowing them to customize the degree to fit their requirements and areas of interest.

Why study in United Kingdom?

A superior academic experience is available to overseas students in the UK. It has everything you need to realize your potential, from renowned universities to cutting-edge teaching methods and the brilliant faculty that provide them.

Some of history's most influential thinkers have chosen to live in the UK. If you want to do great things, the UK is the perfect place to study because one in four world leaders attended university there.

Here are some benefits of studying in the UK:

- **The UK is home to top universities**: The best universities in the world include those in the United Kingdom. In fact, eight UK universities are placed among the top 50 universities worldwide in the QS World University Rankings 2021.
- **It's incredibly diverse:** About 9.5 million individuals, or 14% of the population in the UK, were born abroad. This implies that international students who relocate to the UK may have the chance to experience a wide variety of cultures and meet friends from all over the world.

This is particularly valid if you're relocating to London, where 35% of people were born outside of the UK. Even more, you'll probably be able to maintain a solid connection to your culture by participating in local activities or dining at establishments serving cuisine from your country of origin, which might lessen the effects of homesickness and culture shock.

- **There is support for overseas students:** There is a lot of assistance available for international students in the UK. You might do this online, through your university, or with the help of your local government. For instance, each institution has a department dedicated to serving the requirements of overseas students and providing information on costs, housing options, academic help, etc. Before applying to a university, you might contact this office. The UK Council for Foreign Student Affairs, an organization that advises international students, has a wealth of valuable resources on its website, including information on immigration, accommodation, and mental health.

- **Studying in the UK will improve your English skills** What better country than the UK, the birthplace of the language, to improve your English? You will have the opportunity to hear a variety of British accents while studying in the UK, including English, Irish, Scottish, and Welsh, all of which may sound different depending on where you are. You'll hear many English dialects worldwide since the UK is so varied, offering you a real-world listening experience you might not get at home.

- There are job opportunities after graduation: The government announced in March this year that the Graduate Route will soon be accepting applications. This change is expected to encourage even more students to study in the UK. International students pursuing bachelors, masters, and doctoral degrees can request extensions to remain in the country for an additional two years after graduation beginning in July. This makes it simpler for recent graduates to settle and start professions in the UK. Additionally, there are several employment options, mainly if you work in one of the professions on the UK's Shortage Occupation List. The UK government aggressively recruits experts from overseas for these posts since there is a scarcity of nurses, pharmacists, teachers, engineers, and other professionals in the country.

- **It's a great place to live:** What is life like in the UK, then? Pretty good, according to the OECD Better Life Index. People in the UK gave a 6.8 out of 10 rating to their general level of happiness with life (which is higher than the OECD average). The UK also performs better than average in employment, education, skills, and social connections, which may be significant to prospective overseas students.

- **Finally, you'll have fun**: International students may discover global student cities in the UK, including London, Glasgow, Manchester, and Nottingham. You could wish to check out your new cities top-notch art galleries and museums or take advantage of the UK's vibrant scene during university student evenings. You will see historic castles, discover cliff sides, and travel through scenic villages. Most importantly, you'll make friends worldwide and enjoy exploring the UK with them.

How to study in UK

You have the chance to develop the knowledge, perspective, and confidence you need to reach your full potential by coming to the UK to study. We will walk you through every step of the simple process of applying to study in the UK.

1. **Decide on a university or college and course:** It is vital to study as much as possible about the variety of courses, schools, and institutions available and compare them to ensure that you select the course that is ideal for you and what you want to achieve. It's also critical to review the prerequisites for the course. The course profiles on the institutions' websites might be used for this. You may ask the institution directly if you have any queries, and they will be more than pleased to assist you in locating the data you want.

2. **Register and apply:** Applying to undergraduate programs in the UK is straightforward. You only need to register once, through UCAS, to be considered for admission to all UK schools and universities (Universities and Colleges Admissions Service).

4. **Accept your offer:** If you have received an offer to study, your university or institution will contact you (often by email) to let you know. You may quickly check the progress of your application at any moment if you submit it through UCAS. Congratulations if you receive an unconditional offer of employment! You already have a place to stay so that you may accept. The position is yours if you are approved with a conditional offer, provided that you fulfill a few further criteria. Achieving specific test

scores or grades in the English language might be this. Before receiving your offer for some courses, you could be requested to attend an interview, which may be conducted over the phone or occasionally in person.

5. **Arrange funds:** The moment to set up funds is right now. One of the several scholarships offered to aid with the expense of your study may be accessible to you.

6. **Apply for a visa:** You'll probably require a visa if you're an overseas student enrolling in a program in the UK.

7. **Prepare for your stay:** It's time to start packing after you receive your offer and visa. Now is the time to start thinking about travel, lodging, and anything else you'll need to make the most of your stay in the UK.

Study in the UK requirements

Let's look at the list of prerequisites for studying in the UK before examining why it is still the most popular choice for international students. The UK is, without a doubt, the most sought-after foreign location for higher education worldwide. For international students, the nation provides a variety of specializations at various entrance levels, dynamic campus life, and a global experience. Over 300 institutions, many of which are among the best in the world and have the lowest acceptance rates, are in the UK. It provides inexpensive housing, scholarships, top-notch post-study job options, and high-quality education.

English Language Proficiency Tests

English Proficiency Tests are the most significant and typical prerequisites for studying in the UK.

International students must demonstrate their English language proficiency for all universities and courses by submitting their test results for exams like the International English Language Testing System (IELTS), the Test of English as a Foreign Language (TOEFL), and the Pearson Test of English Academic (PTE Academic).

Students may also submit Duolingo English Assessments, Cambridge Certificate of Proficiency in English (CPE), and Trinity Secure English Language Tests in addition to the frequently approved English language tests for admissions (SELTs).

Entry Requirements to Study in the UK

After graduating from high school, students who desire to continue further education in the UK must complete their 10+2 education from an accredited Indian institution and meet the minimum grades and admissions criteria for the program and university of their choice. The following is a list of prerequisites for undergraduate studies in the UK:

- Certificate for completing the 10+2 program with the required minimum grades from an accredited Indian university.
- Original academic records from prior institutes of higher learning.
- Statement of purpose;
- Letters of recommendation;
- Results of English proficiency exams;
- A passport or other form of photo identification;
- Bank statements as evidence of financial resources; and
- Student visa;
- Offer letter

Offer Letter for the UK

An offer letter is one of the key prerequisites for studying in the UK. Before extending an offer letter to a student, UK institutions carefully review each application form and thoroughly examine any supporting documentation. Offer letters come in two varieties: conditional and unconditional. The condition letter is sent by the university when a student has not completed all of the prerequisites for enrolling in the program and must do so to be admitted, which is how the two letters vary. When a student completes all the admission requirements to study in the UK and must pay the confirmation/course fees to be successfully admitted to the institution, the university extends an unconditional letter.

Popular intakes

There are two main intakes in the UK: January/February and September. Some universities in the UK additionally offer an April/May (summer) admission in addition to these two main intakes.

Education System

The United Kingdom (UK) is well known for its top-notch educational standards, engaging teaching methods, renowned universities, and high levels of student satisfaction. Universities in the UK regularly place highly in international university league tables as the Academic Ranking of World Universities, Times Higher Education Ranking, and QS World Rankings. Additionally, degrees acquired nationwide are accepted worldwide and are sought by employers everywhere.

At the pinnacle of research and development, the UK gives students a wide range of opportunities to develop critical and analytical thinking.

Credit system in the UK

The Credit Accumulation and Transfer Scheme (CATS) is the standard credit system in the United Kingdom. The common number of CATS credits for a complete academic year is 120, and grades are often expressed as percentages (i.e., 0-100). In addition to CATS, most UK colleges also employ the European ECTS system.

Cost of studying and living in the UK

Some of the oldest institutions in the world, including the London School of Economics and Political Science, the University of Cambridge, and the University of Oxford, are located in the United Kingdom. Many students who enrol in these colleges each year intend to pursue their dream careers in the glimmering UK capitals of London, Dublin, Glasgow, and Edinburgh. Although these locations are home to some of the best institutions in the world, it is expensive for overseas students to study and live in the UK.

Another significant factor that significantly raises the price of UK study for Indian students is housing.

- **Universityhousing:**Most institutions provide on-campus or affordable housing for overseas students. This can be obtained at no additional

cost as part of your offer or for a fee. The greatest and least expensive solutions are typically found in university residence halls.
- **Private housing:** If you decide to live in a private house, look for housing options near your university. You can often find a suitable location to live and study for £350 to £550 (Rs. 31000 to Rs. 49000) each month. London is the most costly of these cities in the UK. However, costs might vary.

Scholarships to study in the UK

A wide variety of UK scholarships and fellowships are available for Indian students from the UK government and universities. All prospective students who want to enrol in a full-time study program in any field are eligible to use these financial assistance resources.

What are the criteria for applying for scholarships for studying abroad?

Researching the nation and institution where you intend to pursue higher education is the first and most crucial step in applying for a study abroad program. It would help if you began looking for scholarships for Indian students from UK colleges. Scholarships can differ based on several variables. Indian students may qualify for national, program, course, university, or area-specific scholarships. In addition, there are grants or scholarships financed by the government that students may apply for to pursue higher education in the UK and scholarships for overseas students provided by several organizations.

What kind of expenses are covered under scholarships for studying abroad?

Scholarships often reduce the overall cost of tuition, but some may also provide living costs, travel expenses, or visa fees, depending on the applicant's academic record and background. The British Council and other affiliated organizations administer these scholarship programs and other financial help.

The top ten scholarships for Indian students who want to continue their studies in the UK are as follows:

1. Chevening Scholarships for Indian and International Students
2. Rhodes Scholarships
3. Erasmus Mundus

4. Commonwealth Scholarship and Fellowship
5. GREAT Scholarships
6. Dr. Manmohan Singh Scholarships
7. Commonwealth Scholarship and Fellowship Plan – 2014
8. Goa Education Trust Scholarships
9. Charles Wallace India Trust Scholarships
10. Sir Ratan Tata Scholarships
11. Hornby Scholarships
12. Inlaks Scholarships

Top universities in the UK

1. University of Oxford
2. University of Cambridge
3. Imperial College London
4. UCL (University College London)
5. University of Edinburgh
6. The University of Manchester
7. King's College London (KCL)
8. London School of Economics and PoliticalScience (LSE)
9. University of Bristol
10. The University of Warwick

Course options in the UK

1. Business Analytics
2. Management (MBA and MIM)
3. Computer Science and Information Technology
4. Medicine
5. Nursing
6. Law
7. Architecture and Construction Management
8. Engineering
9. Fashion and Interior Design

How to apply for a study visa in the UK?

The UK is a fantastic destination to live and study, but before you start packing your bags, you should probably apply for a UK study visa.

Who requires a student visa for the UK?

You'll probably require a student visa if you're an overseas student intending to attend school in the UK. The only exceptions to this rule are citizens of Switzerland and the EEA nations, who don't require a visa to enter the UK.

What are the UK student visa requirements you need to meet?

You must fulfill several conditions to successfully apply for a UK student visa. These consist of:

- A full-time course spot has been given to you by an institution that qualifies (i.e., the university must be one of the authorized Tier 4 sponsors for the Student Route Visa).
- You are literate in English (both written and spoken)
- You have enough money to cover the course's cost and the support of any dependents you may have.

Which type of visa do you need to apply for?

There are three main types of UK student visas:

- Student route visa (formerly known as the Tier 4 General student visa)
- Child Student visa (also Tier 4)
- Short-term study visa.

You should apply for a Student route visa (formerly called a Tier 4 General Student visa), if:

- You'll be enrolled in a course at a university or college for more than six months.
- You'll spend more than 11 months enrolled in an English language course.

Apply for a child study visa if the aforementioned applies to you and you are under 18. Short-term study visas cover English language courses that last less than a year.

How to apply for a UK student visa?

1. Check if you need to apply for a student visa in the UK. On the government's website, you may accomplish this.
2. Prepare all of your documents. These consist of your passport, a current photo and fingerprints (taken at a visa application facility), a job offer, documentation of your financial stability (bank statements), and if you don't already have it, evidence of your English language proficiency.
3. Submit an online application through the UK for a Student Route Visa (formerly the Tier 4 General Student Visa).

How long will it take to get UK study visa?

You may anticipate hearing back on your application in 21 days due to the three-week maximum processing period for UK visas. Including the required paperwork with your registration can help you avoid delays.

Submit your application as soon as possible (i.e., as soon as you've prepared your other papers and gotten confirmation of your admission from the school), as the UK student visa application procedure isn't especially rapid. You cannot, however, apply more than three months before the start of your course.

You'll be able to start packing and getting ready for your study as soon as your application for a UK student visa is accepted. Your academic career is about to create an exciting new chapter!

Study pathways to permanent residence (PR)

A viable alternative for staying in the UK after graduation is to get a job. The UK is open to hiring the most talented foreigners after they have earned a degree. Students can apply for a work permit after their studies in the UK. A two- year Post Student Work Visa is a big perk for international students (PSW).

However, it should be highlighted that only those with tier- 2 visas are eligible for permanent work in the UK. Once they have finished their study, international students can apply for a Tier-2 visa. A UK Tier 2 visa is a work visa that permits the bearer to employment in the UK.

The students can seek permanent work in the UK once they have obtained a tier-2 visa. After working graduate employment for five full years, you can apply for a permanent residence card in the UK. The candidate must get an "indefinite leave to remain (ILR) Visa" to become a permanent resident. The ILR visa in the UK may be obtained with the support of full-time work, a solid moral code, and a clean criminal record.

In addition to passing a recognized English language competence test, you must pass the test of Life in the UK. An ILR visa application might take up to 6 months to complete. The following information is gathered for the ILR:

- A current passport
- 2 passport-size color photographs
- Digital prints of all the 10 fingers
- Signature
- Name
- Date and place of birth
- Present immigration status
- Present studying or working status

If you meet all of the criteria listed above, it is possible for Indian and other overseas students to get permanent residency in the UK. It is a fantastic opportunity for overseas students to make a lasting change in their lives.

৪৹

IV
Your study abroad checklist

You've now been accepted into a programme at the foreign university of your choice, and you're preparing to embark on your new life as an international student. Utilize our study abroad check list to make sure you're ready as you wait for the summer to end and the new semester to start.

It is imperative that you take into account the necessary bureaucratic requirements, like travel insurance, that will ensure your time abroad runs as smoothly as possible, regardless of whether you are studying abroad for a month, a semester, an academic year, or a whole degree.

Your passport

Of course, you won't forget your passport. However, in the months prior to your study abroad program, you should determine whether your passport will remain valid for the duration of your travels.

Make sure you factor extra travel time and an additional six months into your study period because many countries will want you to have at least six months on your passport after your studies are up in order to apply for visas.

Figure 4.1: Passport

If you need to renew your passport, do it right now to avoid being without one when the semester begins. Regional differences in processing times result in delays of up to six weeks.

The last thing you want to deal with when travelling to a fascinating new place is dealing with embassy visits, lineups, and a lot more paperwork if you wait until you're abroad to renew your passport.

A student visa

You could require a student visa to stay in the country for the duration of your studies, depending on the study location you've chosen. An accredited university will typically assist with the student visa application if you enroll there for an undergraduate degree. Make sure to ask because this isn't always the case. Start working on getting your student visa on your own if no help is offered.

Figure 4.2: Student Visa

To accomplish this, get in touch with the embassy or university bureau consultant; you could be asked to show up for a scheduled appointment as part of the student visa application process.

Finances

Make sure you have enough money in your bank account to cover the cost of your vacation.

Carry local cash, but don't solely rely on it or withdraw large amounts at once. Since currency rates aren't usually advantageous at airports, make careful to convert your money before leaving. Typically, you may accomplish this at your neighborhood bank, travel companies, bureaus of exchange, post offices, grocery stores, or even a specialized online retailer. You can use tools for price comparison, such as Moneysupermarket, to find the best offers.

Figure 4.3: Finance

You should have a bank account that you can access not only with cash but also with cash cards, credit cards, local ATMs, and foreign bank branches. Although the majority of significant banks are acknowledged globally, you can be assessed a modest fee each time you use your card to make a withdrawal or a payment. To prevent having your card banned, make sure your card is valid for the duration of your trip and that you notify your bank of your plans before leaving.

You must be careful with how you spend your money once you have determined how you will obtain it while you are away. Whether you're sustaining yourself through personal savings, a student loan, a scholarship, or cash from a part-time job, maintaining a budget is one of the best and most challenging things you can do to prevent going broke at the end of each term.

Before you depart, make a list of all your expenses, including everything from hotel to daily meals and entertainment. Determine how much money you'll need each week, and if it isn't enough, think about reducing you're spending on non-essentials or exploring other financing options.

International student scholarships

You might want to look into international student scholarships to see whether you are eligible for additional funding for your study, regardless of how uneasy all this talk of money makes you feel.

Your new university's website, which will give you details on all of their many student scholarships, grants, and bursaries, should be your first point of call. Many of these scholarships are subject-specific, need-based, or restricted to high achievers or underrepresented groups of students. If your institution is unable to offer you anything, an alternative is outside finance. For instance, International Scholarships offers thorough lists of internationally sponsored student scholarships.

However, be sure to conduct thorough research before leaving for college because all student grants are eagerly sought after. You'll have to work really hard and remember application deadlines.

International Student Identity Card (ISIC)

The Foreign Student Identity Card (ISIC), which offers reductions on goods and services globally, should be on every international student's study abroad check list. You can get discounts on international calling cards, travel insurance, public transit, and a range of other services, such as phone repairs and Segway tours, if you visit the International Student Identity Card website to determine if it's perfect for you.

As an international student, you may need assistance with a variety of travel-related issues. The International Student Travel Confederation, which developed the International Student Identity Card (ISIC), has offices in 106 nations.

Travel insurance

Although it may be an unnecessary cost, travel insurance is essential. For a small one-time fee, travel insurance can protect you if anything goes wrong while you're studying, including sickness, accident, or theft, and will stop you from having to spend your whole life's savings on medical bills. You may be asked to provide documentation proving that you have adequate coverage because many countries demand that international students purchase health insurance.

Medical

Before departing from home, it is a good idea to contact your doctor for a thorough physical examination and to make sure you have received all the necessary vaccinations for the study location you have chosen. These vaccinations will be expensive in remote locations, but be assured that your doctor will let you know if they're absolutely necessary.

If you need ongoing care while you're away, make sure your doctor provides a copy of your medical records to your destination. You should allow additional time to obtain your prescription before your medication expires because foreign prescriptions are not always honored.

Language

If you chose to study abroad in a country where the language spoken is not your native tongue, do not worry. The majority of people in Asia and many European nations are at least Basic English speakers. Regardless, you should think about enrolling in some language classes prior to departure so that you may interact and fully immerse yourself in the local culture.

Learning a language used to require signing up for an evening class or reading/listening to a variety of "teach yourself" materials, but nowadays, smartphone apps like Duolingo offer thorough language learning techniques that you can pick up on your own time, with a mix of listening, speaking, and writing to help you develop a more rounded knowledge before you leave.

Bring a phrasebook if you must leave your smartphone at home. Respectfully interacting with people will surely be helpful, particularly if you get lost in a new town or city!

Travel

Every student should place the ability to travel widely and learn about their host country's culture at the top of their priority list when considering studying abroad. In order to travel on a budget, you must not only reserve your initial tickets in advance (including your return!), but you need also think about researching how to get around after you are at your destination.

Since it enables you to compare transportation costs around the world, the internet is a useful tool in this situation. Buying a railcard and bus or coach passes may be advantageous if you frequently take trains.

You won't need to use any of your trip budget if you find deals like these before leaving home. However, be sure you only buy what you actually need!

Essential step

You have a programme starting soon, but are you ready for it yet? We'll show you how to get ready for an international study programme, so don't worry.

The eight steps listed below might help you become familiar with the procedure and be prepared to take it on.

1. **Gather documentation:** You'll see that there are many forms, papers, and applications needed for studying abroad. You should therefore be exceedingly methodical when acquiring them. You must first have a valid passport in order to travel anyplace in the world. If you do, kudos to you! If not, you must get in touch with your neighborhood embassy to find out how to apply for one. You can also need a student visa to enter the country you're visiting, depending on the country. The process is typically simple because each nation's official website offers thorough instructions. For instance, you can check the application requirements on the Government of Canada website if you want to study in Canada. The most frequent paperwork required for study abroad is real passport; a student visa; health insurance; a letter of confirmation from your school; personal identifying numbers; and financial documentation.

2. **Arrange accommodations:** The subsequent steps of preparing for your study abroad will be lot simpler once you have sorted and organized your paper documentation. It's wonderful to be accepted to a university, but now you have to decide where you will live while you study abroad. You must first be aware of the differences between living off-campus and on-campus in order to make an informed choice. This decision will largely be influenced by personal preferences. Since there are no curfews or other limitations, you can live alone, become more independent, and choose where you want to live, according to some students who live off campus. This option, however, typically costs more because rent and transportation expenses have gone up. Finding roommates and making friends is also more challenging.

3. **Speak to a doctor:** Spending four years outside of your own country is typically required to earn a bachelor's degree overseas. You should visit

a doctor for blood work, check-up exams, and other essential treatments in order to stay healthy in the new country. It is always better to be safe than sorry! Being continuously on the move and attempting to figure out multiple things at once when travelling requires you to be in the best physical condition possible. When you're away from friends and family, you won't have the same support, and hospitals can have different policies, which could make getting sick more difficult.

4. **Buy your airline ticket:** This one should go without saying; you must, of course, buy your plane ticket before taking out, but did you know that prices vary significantly depending on a number of factors, including the time, day, airline, and website you use? If you wish to study abroad on a tight budget, keep in mind that the best time to make your travel arrangements is three months in advance. Some people could be picky about their flight times, but in order to get the best deal, you must be willing to change the time and even the day. It's a great idea to purchase international travel insurance to help with unforeseen medical expenses! Even if it costs between 4% and 10% of your total travel expenses, it is still a wise investment that could end up saving you thousands of dollars. For instance, if your vacation cost $5,000, your travel insurance will probably cost between $250 and $500.

5. **Examine the location:** Research and learning are two more things you should do before studying abroad. Spend some time before your trip learning about the locals, their culture, and any issues the country may be facing that could affect your travel plans. You might feel more at ease if you are familiar with the culture, investigate the local cuisine, study the maps and areas, and study the language. When you go there, you can feel bewildered and run across unexpected things, but doing some homework can help you feel less shocked. In addition, look for banks close to your residence in a foreign country and find out what is required to create a bank account as an international student. You desire the security of your funds there!

6. **Join a group on Facebook:** Let's face it: if you don't meet the right people, studying abroad might not be as pleasurable. Depending on your preferences, you can join Facebook groups with locals or international students to fully immerse yourself in the culture and avoid feeling lonely. In any case, you will make new friends, expand your network, enhance your communication abilities, and avoid loneliness. Although there are other ways to make friends abroad, this is the best strategy before you go.

7. **Mentally readjust yourself:** International students encounter a range of emotional problems when studying abroad, including homesickness, culture shock, loneliness, and anxiety. Even if you can expect some challenging times, it's more important that you know how to handle them than anything else. Instead of second-guessing or scrapping your plans to study abroad, you should put your attention on developing your personality so that you can be flexible and prepared to deal with any issues that might emerge.

8. **Get your things ready:** Packing your bags is still to come, which is the most exciting part! Check the weather in the area where you intend to study before you do so you can pack appropriately. Additionally, confirm that you have the proper number of bags and are aware of any weight restrictions.

Visa requirement and processing

Student visas are issued to applicants whose primary purpose for travelling to a foreign country is to pursue education, as the name suggests. Obviously, even though admission to the college is essential, these legal documents will prevent you from achieving any of your objectives. Immigration regulations are in place in every country. Apart from studying there, each visa's activity restrictions, allowed sources of payment, and documentation requirements are all subject to change. All applications for student visas share several other notable similarities.

What is a visa?

A visa is an official form of identification for travel. The visa that is often stamped or adhered to the bearer's passport enables him to visit a foreign nation legally. There are numerous varieties of visas. To begin with, there are different types of visas available for persons who want to travel for pleasure, such as the Tourist Visa, Student Visa, and so forth.

When should you apply for a Student Visa? Planning is absolutely essential when studying abroad. It is always advisable for students to organize their admissions/application process backwards, starting with the university deadlines. According to university regulation, students must take the English eligibility tests and have the necessary paperwork in order for their applications to be processed quickly. Therefore, to avoid any last-minute rush, students are generally urged to apply 1-3 months in advance. Candidates should allow an additional two months for the process because applications for financial aid, scholarships, and student loans take longer.

What type of visa do you need?

Student visas are frequently categorized based on two main grounds of distinction.

1. **Classification of Student Visas Depending on Program Length:** The nations frequently categories student visas into short- term student visas and long-term student visas depending on the length of the program the applicant is planned to enroll in. Students who want to enroll in a short course of a language or a diploma certificate course sometimes receive short-term visas, and the total period is frequently only 90 days (3 months). On the other hand, students who intend to enroll in degree programs lasting more than three months are granted long- term visas. These might include brief certificate programs of six months or internships. This broad categorization is common throughout the nations of the European Union.

2. **Classification of Student Visas Depending on Program/Student:** Some nation's categories student visas based on the type of student, regardless of the length of the course. Depending on the degree level (undergraduate, graduate, or doctorate), exchange student status, or student applying for a vocational or diploma program, this could apply. In general, these visas are partly related to tenure because they depend on the type the student is seeking for, of course. The length of the program would not, however, be the first point of distinction in these categories. If you're an exchange student, for example, you might be there for three months or three years, but the categorization would still be dependent on the type of student and not the length of stay.

Documents required for student visa application

Every country has a distinct list of documents, depending on its immigration regulations. The list is generic, despite the fact that the precise requirements change in terms of actual phrases. There are, however, two documents that you will undoubtedly need.

Valid passport

The main requirement is this. Although you would need a current passport, you should be aware that different nations may have varied requirements regarding the passport's validity. When applying for a student visa, several nations may require that you have validity through the completion of the term. On the other hand, some might accept your application but ask that you have a validity that goes beyond the length of time you plan to stay in the nation. Additionally, make sure your passport has at least two blank pages available for stamping a visa. It's vital to keep in mindthat you will still need to submit copies of all exp ired passports if you have any.

Proof of a bonafide Student

You must be able to demonstrate that you are a legitimate student if you are applying for any category of student visa, regardless of the nation to which you are applying. This is frequently done by presenting admissions documentation from a school in that nation.

Financial lucidity

Most nations would want you to show that you have the financial means to not only pay for your education and college costs, but also to stay in that nation for the duration of your chosen study period. While many nations have a set quantity of money they must have, some have broader, more detailed rules.

For instance, a minimal standard of living is determined according to government regulations in various European nations (such as Germany, the Netherlands, etc.). Accordingly, students applying for student visas in these nations must show proof that the required amount is on hand in the form of ready cash.

Language proficiency

Proof that you can speak in the language that will be your medium of instruction is another thing that may be necessary in different nations. Since the majority of students want to study in English-speaking nations, most of them would need you to present documentation of your ability to communicate in English, both verbally and in writing. A minimum score requirement for different English Language Tests like the TOEFL, IELTS, and/or PTE is often how this is accomplished. As a result, if you want to enroll in a course in any other language, such German, you must present certification in accordance with the CEFR Certified Levels.

While institutions may accept either or both of the aforementioned tests, it is crucial to know that sometimes there are fixed requirements for visas. It is crucial that a student determine whether or not the country's immigration department recognizes the English Language Test before taking it. Additionally, a minimum score is frequently required by visa guidelines for many nations. Universities may admit students with lower test scores, but visas won't be approved until the minimal requirement is satisfied.

Depending on the nation you are applying to, the whole list could vary. While some nations may need medical documentation, others might demand a blocked account. An SOP is required in many nations.

Popular scholarships for studying abroad

Gaining a quality education in top international universities is a dream for many aspirants, however, arranging funds can prove to be a major hurdle to realizing those dreams. To overcome this hindrance, many organizations, universities and governments give scholarships to talented students, so, they are not denied quality education. Below we have provided a list of top international scholarships which students can avail themselves to pursue higher education abroad.

1. Global StudyAwards
2. London BusinessSchool FundScholarships
3. Ontario GraduateScholarship-Other MasterPrograms
4. Central Sector
5. Scheme ofNationalOverseasScholarship forSC etc.
6. Erasmus MundusJoint Mastersscholarships

7. <u>Heinrich BollScholarships forUndergraduates,Graduates, andPhD Students</u>

What is the process for applying for a student visa?

When your university extends a letter of acceptance to you, the procedure for applying for a student visa begins. Students must start the visa application process as soon as they receive their admission letter. Candidates have two options for applying for their visas:

- **Online visa application process:** This is the more practical method of applying for a student visa, requiring only the creation of a student profile. All of the forms must be completed accurately by the student and are available online.
- **Offline visa application process:** Under the offline visa application process, applicants must download the necessary forms, complete them, and submit them to the appropriate authorities.

The Visa Application Fee is paid in the next stage. Each applicant would need to pay a fee for a student visa in order to submit an application. The final step would be for the student to submit his application and any supporting materials.

Requirements for visa extension

A visa is granted for a set amount of time. In the event that your study permit expires prior to the conclusion of your course of study (program), you must apply for a renewal. The ideal time to apply is at least 30 days prior to the expiration of your current permit. Candidates have the option of applying online or via mail.

ৰু

V

Fast track method

To simplify the process for students to study abroad, I have created a fast track method, which is a one stop solution to all your needs for studying abroad, a platform called University Bureau, you can access the platform at https://universitybureau.com/ University Bureau, an Overseas student Recruitment AI-Enabled Platform.

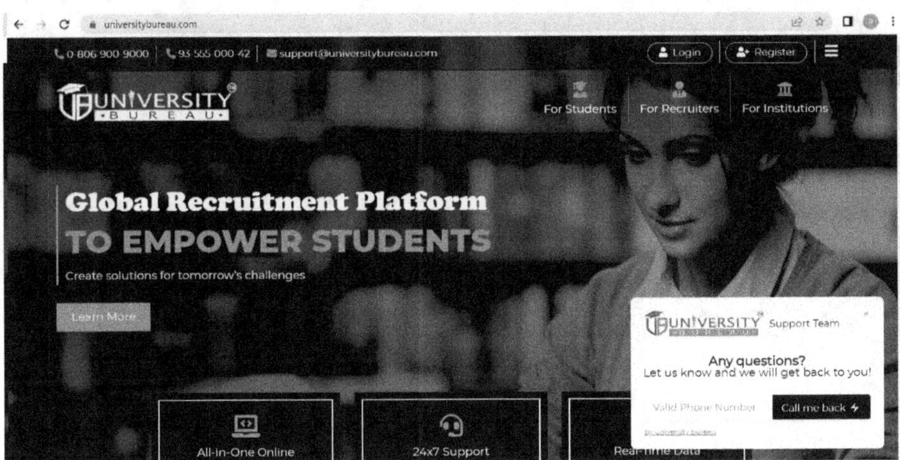

Figure 5.1: University Bureau home page

We provide a recruitment platform, providing End to End support from research to admission to visa and arrival at your dream Institute. We guide you at every step of the way 24x7!

Dream-Achieve-Success-Grow

Find everything you need on one platform: 5,000+ recruiters & 1,500+ institutions globally through one marketplace.

We guide, build confidence and help students worldwide to study and get the best international education. We provide a recruitment platform which enables institutions and recruitment agents to find and transact with each other, seamlessly.

Think, approach us for getting the best out of the best course, take a step ahead and celebrate your win with us.

University Bureau aims to simplify your search to study abroad and streamline the application-acceptance process by connecting international students, recruitment partners, and academic institutions on one platform.

Features of University Bureau

- University Bureau makes your search easy to study abroad, simplifies your application filing, and makes your application acceptance process successful. We connect international students, recruitment partners (5,000+), and academic institutions (1,500+) on one platform across Canada, the United States, the United Kingdom, and Australia.
- We provide you Quality Compliance and Visa (QCV) team to conduct in-depth checks on all visa and course applications by using intuitive automation tools. We aim to make the application process smooth and stress-free for students, recruiters and universities by providing 1- on-1 support worldwide.
- We provide student portal to recruiters, which saves recruiters time and gives students a seamless counselling experience. With us, students will understand their application funnel and data is organized in one secure place by following a Privacy Compliance Program aligned with the General Data Protection Regulation.

Why University Bureau?

Choose us for the best assistance to discover programs and institutions, get the best options for you, and prepare everything for easy submission of your applications.

- **Admission Officer:** Select your admission officer from our platform and get guidance from creating your profile to applying to multiple institutions and course selection from over 50,000+ programs.
- **IELTS:** We have a team of the world's best trainers from where you can select your trainer by using our platform to prepare yourself for the IELTS exam.
- **Financial Officer:** Our financial officers will provide you with exclusive scholarships and good financial support options.
- **Visa Assistance:** Our top-rated certified visa counselor will help you at every step of the visa process, from application filing to document preparation. You can select a top-rated counselor at your convenience.
- **Continuous Support:** We have a team of over 5,000+ recruiters, certified experts for 1-on-1 support around the world.

How University Bureau works?

We built a relationship with students on Trust and Credibility. UB will take a short survey, filter & select programs and institute for you. Then we will help you to complete your profile, pay fees, and submit documents. Once the institute reviews your application and issues an acceptance letter then our expert recruiter will guide you through the visa application process. You are now ready to board your flight and start your dream journey.

So, what are you waiting for contact university bureau at 0-806-900-9000 or 93-555-000-42

Also, you can drop an email on: support@universitybureau.com

Our expert counselors will guide you the process for studying abroad and help you to achieve your dreams.

About University Bureau

"University Bureau," an AI-enabled platform for recruiting international students for higher education (https://universitybureau.com/). Our AI feature identifies the document and provides automated document verification. The site can validate IDs, academic transcripts, employment history, fraud detection, and so on.

We are a global recruitment platform that aims to give students the tools they need to solve today's problems.

Our head office is in California, USA, while our Asia office is in Delhi/NCR, India. Per intake, we typically recruit 2000–2500 students worldwide.

We currently have more than 1500 channel partners in our portfolio, spread out over India and the APAC area, who offer services in Nepal, Bangladesh, Bhutan, Vietnam, and India.

We would like to become affiliated with your prestigious organization to recruit students in your colleges from India and the APAC area. We are experts in both marketing and technology. Experts in the admissions process, the VISA process, and other services make up our team. We also have strong internal marketing and IT team.

VI

Worrying about IELTS/ PTE/TOEFL

Learn IELTS/PTE/TOEFL anytime and anywhere!

The study from home! Yes, you heard it right, with IELTSBureau, prepare your IELTS/PTE/TOEFL exam by studying at home.

To simplify your needs to study abroad along with https://universitybureau.com/ I have created another platform as https://ieltsbureau.com/

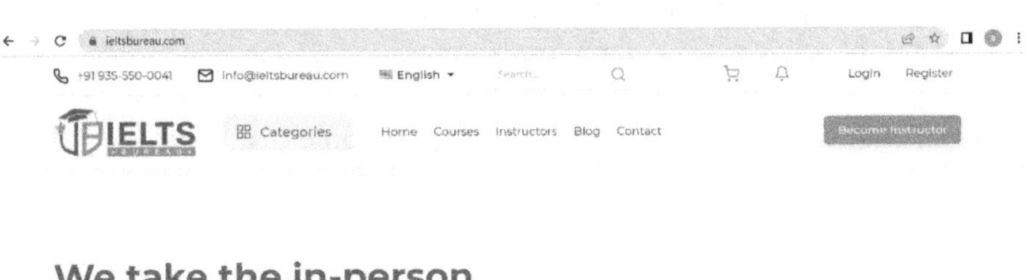

Figure 6.1: IELTS Bureau home page

Are you struggling to get a band 8 or above in an IELTS exam? Or worried about how to prepare for the test that takes you ahead in your journey of studying abroad.

IELTSBureau.com is all that you need. With us, know the little-known strategies and techniques for listening, writing, speaking, and reading; and ace your IELTS/PTE/TOEFL test scores.

Join the first ever study abroad online test preparation portal.

So, kick start your dream to study abroad; IELTSBureau is here to help you to get the best IELTS/PTE/TOEFL score band and experience your dream to study abroad.

You choose your trainer from the pool of the world's best trainers, and we'll do the rest; guide you with your preparation, providing directions and assistance to get the required band for IELTS/PTE/TOEFL exam.

- Get more profound insights into the IELTS/PTE/TOEFL exams
- Pool of IELTS/PTE/TOEFL trainers to select your trainer based on experience, timing, fees
- Connect with our certified faculties LIVE and get all your doubts clear
- End-to-end training
- Webinars every week
- Flexible batch timings
- Get regular practice material and weekly mock tests
- 1:1 speaking and essay evaluations
- Live doubt solving It is as simple as that!

If you want world-class education at an affordable cost, the answer could be IELTSBureau.

About IELTSBureau

An educational experience that covers the needs of both learners and educators

IELTS Bureau is a powerful but simple learning platform that puts a wide choice of expert instructors at your fingertips. Now you can easily prepare for—IELTS, TOEFL, GRE, PTE, and more—whenever and wherever you are.

Pursuing our mission to provide a platform where every learner can access best-in-class instructors and prepare for their test without extra cost or location barriers.

This platform allows learners and instructors to communicate, collaborate, learn, and earn from wherever they are and with whatever device they like.

Whether you want crash IELTS preparation, wish to study for a few months, or need weekend lessons.

Find an instructor that suits your needs and book your first lesson

Connect with the best tutors around the world

We make learning happen for everyone; wherever you are, we are with you.

We know how it feels when you're just starting and need help with your preparation.

Whether you need more balance and flexibility or just want access to dedicated instructors and institutions worldwide, we make it easier for you to start your learning journey...

One-on-one learning experience with top-notch instructors and institutions designed to give you the personal attention you need to achieve your target score.

Whether searching for IELTS, TOEFL, or GRE, we strive to make the process as simple and affordable as possible.

Excellent opportunity to take in the lead-up to your test to make sure you have the confidence you need to ace your test

With no monthly fee, you can find the help you need when you need it.

So, what are you waiting for contact at:

+91 93555 00042

info@ieltsbureau.com

and get one-stop shop for your learning needs.

www.ingramcontent.com/pod-product-compliance
Lightning Source LLC
Chambersburg PA
CBHW071333140726
47996CB00005B/1947